• **Second edition**

CAMBRIDGE

Objective
PET

Louise Hashemi
Barbara Thomas

Workbook with answers

CAMBRIDGE LEARNER CORPUS
REAL ENGLISH GUARANTEE

CAMBRIDGE
UNIVERSITY PRESS

CAMBRIDGE
UNIVERSITY PRESS

University Printing House, Cambridge CB2 8BS, United Kingdom

Cambridge University Press is part of the University of Cambridge.

It furthers the University's mission by disseminating knowledge in the pursuit of education, learning and research at the highest international levels of excellence.

www.cambridge.org
Information on this title: www.cambridge.org/9780521732710

© Cambridge University Press 2010

First published 2003
Second edition published 2010
8th printing 2014

Printed in the United Kingdom by Latimer Trend

A catalogue record for this publication is available from the British Library

ISBN 978-0-521-73268-0 Student's Book without answers with CD-ROM
ISBN 978-0-521-73266-6 Student's Book with answers with CD-ROM
ISBN 978-0-521-73269-7 Teacher's Book
ISBN 978-0-521-73274-1 Audio CDs (3)
ISBN 978-0-521-73270-3 Workbook without answers
ISBN 978-0-521-73271-0 Workbook with answers
ISBN 978-0-521-73272-7 Self-study pack
ISBN 978-0-521-16827-4 For Schools Pack without answers

Cover concept by Dale Tomlinson and designed by David Lawton

Produced by Kamae Design, Oxford

Contents

Unit 1
A question of sport — 4

Unit 2
I'm a friendly person — 6

Unit 3
What's your job? — 8

Unit 4
Let's go out — 10

Unit 5
Wheels and wings — 12

Unit 6
What did you do at school today? — 14

Unit 7
Around town — 16

Unit 8
Let's celebrate — 18

Unit 9
How do you feel? — 20

Unit 10
I look forward to hearing from you — 22

Unit 11
Facts and figures — 24

Unit 12
A good read — 26

Unit 13
A place of my own — 28

Unit 14
What's in fashion? — 30

Unit 15
Risk! — 32

Unit 16
Free time — 34

Unit 17
Next week's episode — 36

Unit 18
Shooting a film — 38

Unit 19
Happy families — 40

Unit 20
So you think you've got talent? — 42

Unit 21
Keep in touch! — 44

Unit 22
Strange but true? — 46

Unit 23
Best friends? — 48

Unit 24
I've got an idea — 50

Unit 25
Shop till you drop — 52

Unit 26
Persuading people — 54

Unit 27
Travellers' tales — 56

Unit 28
What would you do? — 58

Unit 29
What's on the menu? — 60

Unit 30
Blue for a boy, pink for a girl? — 62

Answer key — 65
Acknowledgements — 80

1 A question of sport

Vocabulary

1 Say and write the names of the sports.

a *basketball*

b ....

c ....

d ....

e ....

f ....

g ....

2 Complete these sentences.

a A *helmet* .... is a kind of hat.

b A .... is a kind of bat.

c In snowfering, they use a kind of ....
with a sail.

d In curling, they use special .... and
....

e Bossaball players always .... shorts
and they usually play in the ....

3 Use the words in the box to complete this paragraph.

> fall   cover   wear   ~~bike~~   ice   cycling
> winter   dangerous   steep

I usually go to school on my (a) *bike* .... I like
(b) .... It's not (c) .... because there's
a cycle path. It's a bit (d) .... so I sometimes
walk. In (e) .... there's often (f) .... on
the path. I don't usually (g) .... over, luckily!
But it's cold, so I (h) .... a big coat and I
(i) .... my head.

Grammar

4 These sentences have words in the wrong place.
Mark the correct place.

a Often I play basketball after school.

b There are lots of people usually at the swimming
pool.

c My sister always is happy at weekends.

d Do sometimes your parents play tennis with
you?

e We go horse riding usually with our friends.

f Our dog usually doesn't like playing games, but
he enjoys always football.

g My brother watches never sport on television.

5 Match the endings to their beginnings to make a story. There is sometimes more than one correct answer.

1	Peter always	**a**	does his homework in the café.
2	He often	**b**	helps him.
3	He usually	**c**	knows when Alison helps Peter.
4	Alison sometimes	**d**	makes mistakes.
5	She never	**e**	makes mistakes.
6	Their teacher always	**f**	has lots of homework.

GF page 206

Writing

6 Complete these sentences with true information.

a Footballers always ....

b Tennis players usually ....

c My teacher never ....

d My friends and I often ....

e In this class, we sometimes ....

Exam skills

Reading Part 1

Look at the text in each question.
What does it say?
Mark the correct letter **A**, **B** or **C**.

1

Delete Reply Reply All Forward Print

Hi Mum
The hotel is small but it has a sports club. I play tennis there. We have great football matches on the beach.
Neil

A Neil doesn't like his hotel.
B Neil plays tennis on the beach.
C Neil enjoys playing football.

2

Abby – I can meet you tomorrow after school at the café or later in the city centre. Please phone and say when you're free. Chloe

CONTINUE   MORE

A Chloe wants Abby to phone her.
B Chloe can see Abby before or after school.
C Chloe is not free in the afternoon.

I'm a friendly person

Pronunciation

2 Say these words.

> sun   new   hot

Look at these sentences. Mark the three sounds (/ʌ/ as in *sun*, /juː/ as in *new*, and /ɒ/ as in *hot*) in different ways. Put them into the correct column.

a Few students come to this club on Mondays.

b They listen to pop music and discuss the future.

c Does it cost much to belong to the club?

/ʌ/ sun	/juː/ new	/ɒ/ hot
come	few	on

Vocabulary

3 Complete the sentences with the words in the box.

> shy   ~~independent~~   serious   tidy
> hard-working   busy   friendly   happy

a I like doing things alone. I'm an
   independent person.

b I enjoy meeting new people. I'm a
   .... person.

c I'm studying for exams, I go swimming every day and I often play the guitar with my friends. I'm a .... person.

d I don't like seeing things in the wrong places. I'm a .... person.

e I like reading and talking about politics and art. I'm not interested in pop music or computer games. I'm a ....
   person.

f I've got two jobs. I'm a ....
   person.

g I don't like meeting new people. I'm a
   .... person.

h I smile all the time. I'm a ....
   person.

Grammar

1 Find the mistakes and correct them.

a Martin: Hello, Felix. What ~~do~~ *would* you like to drink?
   Felix: A coffee, please.

b Emily: Does Amy like to go to the disco with us?
   Jack: I think she wants staying at home. She doesn't like the disco.

c My brother would like going to the disco with you but he got homework.

d Tessa: How many children have your sister?
   John: Two – a boy and a girl.

e Grace: Do Paul likes pop music?
   Freya: No, he likes classical music.

f Jenny: What would you like doing on holiday?
   Abdul: Oh, I like walking in the mountains.

↘ GF page 206

4 Complete this email with the words in the box.

watching	like	playing	would	~~want~~
I've	name	I'd	plans	cycling

New Message

File   Edit   View   Insert   Format   Tools   Message   Help

Dear Luca

I (**a**) _want_ to tell you about my (**b**) .... for Saturday. (**c**) .... got a new bicycle. It's red and I can go very fast on it. I (**d**) .... riding it. I also like (**e**) .... computer games with my friends but I don't like (**f**) .... television.

On Saturday, (**g**) .... like to go (**h**) .... with my brother. His (**i**) .... is Keith. (**j**) .... you like to come with us?

See you soon.

Gary

Writing

5 You want to find a friend who's got the same interests as you. Fill in this page from a website.

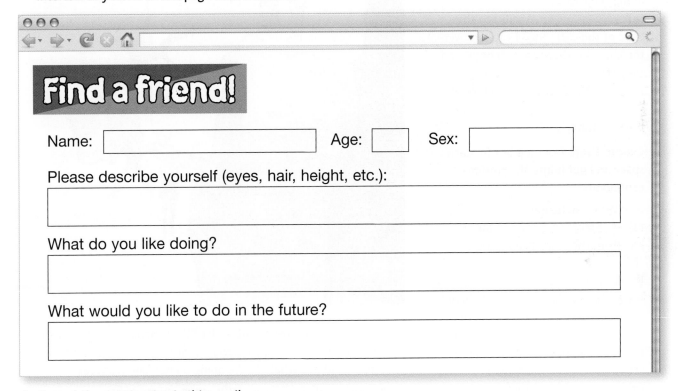

Find a friend!

Name: [＿＿＿＿＿＿＿＿] Age: [＿] Sex: [＿＿＿]

Please describe yourself (eyes, hair, height, etc.):

What do you like doing?

What would you like to do in the future?

6 Correct the punctuation in this email.

I'm
~~im~~ enjoying my holiday in ireland

we swim in the morning and then have lunch at a restaurant called

patricks garden

my parents like visiting museums but i dont

i sometimes drive my parents car to dublin and meet my cousins

there

were flying to america next week

ryan

3 What's your job?

Grammar

1   Here is a radio report about a rescue. Put the verbs into the present continuous.

I (**a**) *'m standing* (stand) near the top of the cliff. I can't see what (**b**) .... (happen) yet. There's a ship in the middle of the bay. It (**c**) .... (not move). A fire engine (**d**) .... (drive) along the road. I (**e**) .... (walk) to the edge of the cliff. Now I can see over the cliff. Yes, there are two boys, and they (**f**) .... (hold) on to a tree. Now some firefighters (**g**) .... (try) to reach the boys, but they can't.

2   Choose a verb from the box for each space and put it into the present continuous.

And now a helicopter (**a**) *is flying* across the bay from the ship. The sailors (**b**) .... from the ship. I think the pilot (**c**) .... for somewhere to land. No, the helicopter (**d**) .... (not), the pilot (**e**) .... the helicopter in the air. The door of the helicopter (**f**) .... A man (**g**) .... under the helicopter. He's beside the boys. Now he (**h**) .... the boys up with him to the helicopter. Now they're all safe in the helicopter. The helicopter (**i**) .... towards the ship. The sailors (**j**) .... and the firefighters (**k**) .... !

hang	~~fly~~	go	keep	land
look	open	smile	take
watch	wave		

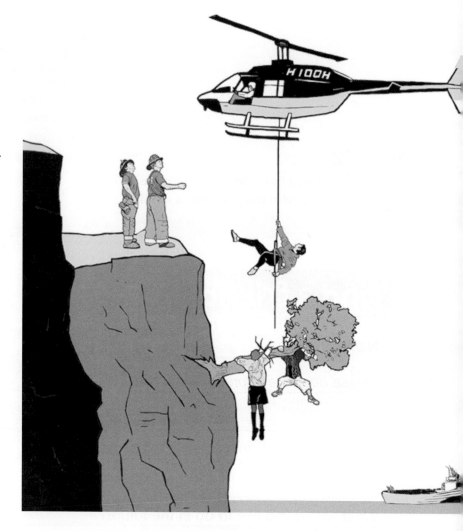

3   Write two sentences about each of these people using the words given. Write one sentence about what they usually do and one sentence about what they're doing on holiday this week.

a work / office   Ula *usually works in an office.* ....
camp / in France
This week she *'s camping in France.* ....

b drive / taxi   Viera ....
play / chess   This week she ....

c play / football   Yuri ....
open / restaurant   This week he ....

d study / laboratory   Zach ....
visit / his family ....

e write / computer games   Tessa ....
study / Chinese ....

f interview / famous people   Amos ....
read books and cook for his family ....

4 Put the verbs into the correct form: present continuous or present simple. Think carefully about the word order.

Brian and his wife have a small shop. This week Brian's in hospital and his sons Steve and Tony are helping their mother to look after the business. Brian is phoning Steve.

Brian: Hello, Steve? Is everything OK?
(a) _Are you doing_ (you/do) everything right?
Steve: Yeah, don't worry, Dad. Everything's great.
Brian: (b) .... (I/count/always) the newspapers before (c) .... (I/open) the shop. (d) .... (you/count) them?
Steve: (e) .... (Mum/count) them right now.
Brian: But (f) .... (your mother/go/always) to the bank before we open the shop.
Steve: It's OK, (g) .... (Tony/go) to the bank now.
Brian: But (h) .... (Tony/put/always) the fruit and vegetables out and he (i) .... (wash) the floor.
Steve: The floor is clean. (j) .... (I/put) the fruit and vegetables out now. (k) .... (I/carry) a box of oranges in one hand and the phone in the other!
Brian: OK. But it's half past eight. (l) .... (We/open/always) at half past eight. (m) .... (You/not/open) the shop on time!
Steve: Dad, (n) .... (I/put) the box of oranges on the shelf. OK? And now (o) .... (I/walk) to the door, and (p) .... (I/open) it.
Brian: Good.
Steve: And (q) .... (some people/come) into the shop.
Brian: And (r) .... (you/not/help) them! Stop talking to me and help them!
Steve: Yes, Dad. Bye.

⤷ GF page 206

5 Complete the answers to these questions.
a Do you play volleyball? Yes, _I do._
b Are you writing notes? No, _I'm not._
c Do your parents enjoy shopping? No, ...
d Is Nigel watching a film? Yes, ...
e Does your sister like ice cream? No, ...
f Are the students playing computer games? Yes, ...
g Do you enjoy skiing? Yes, ...
h Are your friends listening to music? No, ...
i Does Leonie paint good pictures? Yes, ...

Writing

6 Imagine you are doing 'work experience' this week like an English teenager.

Write three sentences about what you usually do and then three sentences about what you are doing this week.

| I usually go to school on weekdays. |
| 1 |
| 2 |
| 3 |
| I'm working in the office of a newspaper this week. |
| 1 |
| 2 |
| 3 |

Vocabulary

7 Put these letters in the correct order to make the names of jobs.
a chamince _mechanic_
b posh sanasistt ....
c naulistjor ....
d airshredres ....
e phrophogater ....
f reingene ....
g leass nerpso ....

4 Let's go out

Vocabulary

1 Find the spelling mistakes in these sentences and correct them.

Wednesday

a I'm starting my new job next ~~Wenesday~~.

b My birthday is on 18 Septembre and my brother's is on 18 Febuary.

c We go to Greece for our holiday every sumer.

d In Augost the city is very quiet.

e Natasha always goes out with her friends on Saterdays.

f This shop is closed tommorrow.

g I never work on 1st Januery.

h On Tuseday and Thusday evenings I play volleyball.

i I'm going to Argentina in Aprile.

2 There are twelve words from Unit 4 in this wordsearch. Can you find them?

P	B	O	S	M	U	S	M	A	G	I	C
H	L	L	P	U	C	R	I	I	M	E	I
I	T	A	D	S	O	W	R	D	A	P	N
N	Q	J	Y	I	M	O	Z	A	T	E	E
T	C	O	N	C	E	R	T	M	R	R	M
E	I	Y	S	A	D	A	M	Y	O	F	A
R	R	G	H	L	Y	A	R	E	C	O	R
V	C	U	A	L	H	P	N	U	K	R	E
A	U	F	B	A	N	D	K	C	C	M	E
L	S	D	E	U	S	R	O	U	E	R	A

Grammar

3 Some students are visiting your school from Italy next week. A student called Maria is staying with your family. Look at the programme for the visit and write to Maria and tell her what is happening each day.

VISIT BY STUDENTS FROM ITALY
Programme

Mon
evening (you) arrive at 10 pm

Tues
(we) visit museums in London
evening (we) see a play at the theatre in London

Wed
(you) spend the day at school
evening (we) go to the cinema

Thurs
(you) do different sports in the activity centre
evening (you) have meal in a restaurant with my family

Fri
morning (you) go shopping
afternoon (we) prepare for a party
evening (we) have a party

Sat
morning (you) leave for an early flight

Dear Maria
We've got a great programme for you!
You are arriving on Monday evening at 10pm.
On Tuesday we ....
....
On Tuesday evening ....
....
....
....
....
....
....
....
....
....
....
....
We're looking forward to meeting you.
Love,

⟳ Corpus spot

4 Here are some sentences by PET students. Most of them have mistakes. Find the mistakes and correct them or write *correct*.

a I arrived ~~on~~ *in* the morning and everybody was asleep.

b He is finishing university on June.

c Why don't we meet tonight on six o'clock?

d The weather is cold at night here.

e We have to work hard but in the weekend we can go shopping.

f Maybe she will come to Spain in Christmas.

g I have a job as a waitress in the weekend.

h I can give it to you in this afternoon.

i This is the ring my grandmother gave me on my 18th birthday.

j I'm going to Paris in 25th March.

5 Fill each of the spaces in this email with one word. If no word is necessary, mark – .

Dear Mum and Dad

I'm writing to tell you what I'm doing. I'm catching a train
(**a**) ......–....... tomorrow to the north. It's very hot here
(**b**) ......*in*........ the summer, so it will be good to have a few days by the sea.

(**c**) .... the weekend I'm visiting a friend called Alison, who lives nearby. She's taking me sailing (**d**) .... Saturday, then (**e**) .... Sunday afternoon we're visiting her family.
I'm coming back here (**f**) .... that evening because I'm hoping to get a job in a café. I'm having an interview with the owner (**g**) .... 7.30 (**h**) ....Monday morning!

The job suits me because I only have to work (**i**) .... the evening, so I can stay in bed till midday.
I'm coming home (**j**) .... June. I have a ticket for a flight
(**k**) .... 26 June but I can change it. I can't wait to see you. And I really want to see my old school friends. I can't believe I last saw them (**l**) .... 2009!
See you soon.

Love,
Megan

↘ GF page 206

Exam skills

Writing Part 2

An English friend of yours called David wants to meet you next Saturday, but you can't see him then.

Write an email to David. In your email, you should

● say why you can't see him

● suggest a different day

● tell him what you would like to do

Write 35–45 words.

Dear David

Grammar

1 Put the words in the box into the correct circle. There are eight words in each circle.

> ~~advice~~ bread chocolate
> country furniture holiday
> information journey
> luggage money motorway
> music shoe toothbrush
> tram wheel

a

some

advice

2 Complete the conversations. Use *a*, *some* or *any*.

Man: I'd like to book (**a**) ......*a*...... single room, please.

Woman: I'm sorry. There aren't (**b**) .... single rooms available tonight but we've got (**c**) .... double rooms.

Man: OK. I'll take (**d**) .... double room.

Girl: Are there (**e**) .... shops in this airport?

Boy: Over there.

Girl: Good. I want to buy (**f**) .... chocolate.

Man: I'm going to the shops to get (**g**) .... bread for breakfast. Do we need (**h**) .... milk?

Woman: We don't need (**i**) .... milk, but we need (**j**) .... coffee.

Man: OK.

Boy: Would you like to go to the concert at the City Hall tonight?

Girl: Yes, but I haven't got (**k**) .... ticket, and I haven't got (**l**) .... money.

Boy: Don't worry. I can give you (**m**) .... money.

3 Complete this email. Use *much, many, a few, a little* or *a lot of*.

Dear Philippe
How are you? I don't have (**a**) ...*much*....... free time now because I'm working on a check-in desk at the airport. I see (**b**) .... people but I don't have (**c**) .... time to talk to them of course because I'm looking at their bags and their tickets. Some people only have (**d**) .... luggage and some have six suitcases! I don't earn (**e**) .... money but I enjoy it. I don't get (**f**) .... weekends off – only one a month usually – but I'm free on Mondays and Tuesdays. That's good because the gym is quiet on Monday mornings – there are only (**g**) .... people there and there aren't (**h**) .... cars on the road, so I'm happy.
See you soon.
Robbie

4 Complete the sentences.

It's very dark.
We need *to turn the light on.*

Do you want to ride on the back
of my motorbike?
You need ....

The room is hot.
I need ....

His clothes are very dirty.
He needs ....

EXHIBITION
FREE

The exhibition is free.
We needn't ....

The table is broken.
She needs ....

FLOUR

I want to make a cake.
I need ....

The door isn't locked.
You don't need ....

5 Complete these sentences with
the correct form of *need*.

a The children are very tired.
They *need* .... to go to
bed.

b My mother ....to
write some letters.

c ....(you) any help
with this exercise.

d I can cook the dinner. You
.... do it.

e My brother is very shy. He
.... to go out and
meet people.

f We ....eat in the
airport. We can have lunch
on the plane.

g My son wants to go karting –
.... (he) a helmet.

⬎ GF page 207

Vocabulary

6 The vowels are missing from
these words. They are all ways
of travelling. Write the words.

a SHP   *ship* ....

b CCH   ....

c TX   ....

d HLCPTR   ....

e MTRBK   ....

f FRRY   ....

g BCYCL   ....

h SCTR   ....

i TRN   ....

j LRRY   ....

What did you do at school today?

Grammar

1 Put the verbs into the past simple. They are all regular verbs.

a I _started_ learning English at primary school. (start)

b My parents .... our house before the visitors .... (tidy) (arrive)

c .... your brother .... the match last night? (enjoy)

d My cat .... onto the table. (not jump)

e The police officer .... my friend. (not arrest)

f .... you .... your teacher to the meeting? (invite)

2 Put the verbs into the past simple. They are all irregular verbs.

a My father _saw_ me in the city centre. (see)

b The concert .... at 8.30. (begin)

c My brother .... coffee for my friends. (make)

d The shop assistant .... happy to help us. (be)

e .... the clowns funny? (be)

f .... you .... shy at the party? (feel)

g We .... any good ideas in that book. (not find)

h .... you .... all your money in town? (spend)

i The manager .... us to leave the club. (tell)

j .... your girlfriend very annoyed? (be)

k Our team .... the match, and we .... very happy about it! (lose) (not be)

3 Use the past simple of the verbs in the box to complete this article about a famous novelist. (Look up any words you don't know in your dictionary.)

~~be~~ be be become die divorce enjoy not go have introduce learn meet work write write

Agatha Christie
– who was she?

Agatha Christie (**a**) _was_ born in England in 1890. She (**b**) .... an American father and an English mother. They (**c**) .... quite rich.

Agatha (**d**) .... to school, but she (**e**) .... reading and she (**f**) .... poems and short stories in notebooks. She also loved parties and dancing.

In 1914 she married her first husband, Archibald Christie. She (**g**) .... about medicines and poisons when she (**h**) .... as a nurse during the First World War. Her first detective novel (**i**) .... *The Mysterious Affair at Styles*. In it, she (**j**) .... her readers to Hercule Poirot, the famous Belgian detective.

Agatha and Archibald (**k**) .... in 1928. Two years later, she (**l**) .... the archaeologist Max Mallowan, in the Middle East. He (**m**) .... her second husband.

Agatha Christie (**n**) .... over 80 novels. She (**o**) .... in 1976.

4 Read this email and choose the correct adjective from each pair.

Delete Reply Reply All Forward Print

We went to a football match yesterday. It was very **(a)** *exciting / excited*. We all shouted and jumped up and down. I felt really **(b)** *tiring / tired* when I arrived home. My girlfriend isn't **(c)** *interesting / interested* in football, so she went to the cinema. She said she saw an **(d)** *amusing / amused* film about a **(e)** *boring / bored* housewife. The woman's husband went to football matches every weekend. His wife met an unusual man who thought football was **(f)** *boring / bored*. I wasn't **(g)** *amusing / amused*.

↘ **GF page 207**

5 In this wordsearch there are sixteen more verbs in the past simple. Can you find them? They go in all directions.

A	B	E	C	A	M	E	E	M	A	D	E
T	B	E	W	B	W	A	R	E	D	E	D
C	F	P	G	O	T	E	A	T	O	O	K
E	L	Q	X	A	Y	P	L	A	M	P	N
F	W	S	A	D	N	P	S	B	I	L	E
D	E	T	C	M	Z	O	T	E	D	I	W
H	R	L	E	D	T	E	U	D	F	I	N
I	E	U	T	F	S	D	D	S	S	T	Y
J	M	N	M	O	O	F	I	H	X	U	E
X	E	A	J	U	L	A	E	O	V	A	W
W	N	R	K	N	R	D	D	B	I	L	T
Z	O	V	V	D	S	I	T	S	K	E	D

Vocabulary

6 Find the odd words out in these lists.

a university <u>uniform</u> secondary school college

b boring nervous embarrassed amazed

c farm airport laptop factory

d historian politician scientist teenager

e boot traffic door window

f music history laboratory maths

Pronunciation

7 Say these verbs aloud and put them into the correct column.

~~ended~~	~~enjoyed~~	~~kicked~~	happened
imagined	included	jumped	liked
needed	opened	travelled	visited
walked	wanted	watched	

/d/ arrived	/t/ helped	/ɪd/ started
enjoyed	kicked	ended

7 Around town

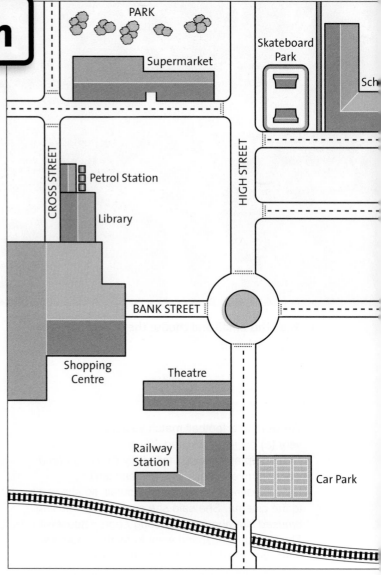

Grammar

1 Make sentences using the words below.

a I / Zac Efron (not famous)
I'm not as famous as Zac Efron.

b the city / the countryside (busy)

....

....

c China / Britain (big)

....

....

d newspapers / magazines (not expensive)

....

....

e hockey / football (not popular)

....

....

f my father / my teacher (old)

....

....

g horses / elephants (not dangerous)

....

....

h a train / a bicycle (fast)

....

....

i I / my best friend (tall)

....

....

2 Complete these sentences with a preposition from the box.

up   down   across   off   ~~around~~   through   over

a We drove *around* the town because there was a traffic jam in the centre.

b The horse jumped .... the gate.

c We walked .... the hill because there was a good view at the top.

d I fell .... the stairs from the top to the bottom but I was OK.

e Never run .... a road without looking.

f He dived .... the rock into the sea.

g We cycled .... the tunnel.

3 Look at the map. Write sentences about the places below using the prepositions in the box.

behind   between   ~~near~~   next to   opposite

a theatre (railway station)
The theatre is near the railway station.

b school (skateboard park)

....

c car park (railway station)

....

d park (supermarket)

....

e library (petrol station, shopping centre)

....

....

↘ GF page 207

Vocabulary

4 Read sentences a–l and fill in the missing words in the square below. Follow the arrows. Each new word uses the last letter of the word before.

a The people who organise the town work in the town _hall_ .

b Stop when the traffic _lights_ are red.

c You can play football in the sports ....

d You can look at paintings and old things in the ....

e You can buy things outdoors in the ....

f A .... is smaller than a city.

g You can dance in a ....

h Buy a ticket and travel around on a ....

i Get some exercise in the .... pool.

j This shop only sells fruit and vegetables. ....

k Find a taxi at the taxi ....

l Buy something to read at the newspaper ....

↓ Start

	↓					←
H						
A		↓			←	
L			↓		←	
L				■		
I				■		
G			→		↑	
H		→				↑
T	→ S				↑	↑

Writing

5 Look at the map again. Complete the directions from:

a the shopping centre to the railway station
Come out of the shopping centre into Bank Street.
....
....
....
....

b the supermarket to the library
Come out of the supermarket and turn right.
....
....
....
....

c the railway station to the skateboard park
Come out of the railway station and turn left.
....
....
....
....

Pronunciation

6 Read these words aloud. Which words contain the sound /ɔː/ as in *more*? Which words contain the sound /aʊ/ as in *town*? Put them into the correct column.

how   walk   house   now   tall   board   found   bought   sport   down

/ɔː/ more	/aʊ/ town
walk	how

Let's celebrate

Grammar

1 Put the verbs into the present perfect tense.

a I *'ve seen* .... this film before. (see)

b Angela .... a cake for your birthday. (make)

c .... you .... your meal? (enjoy)

d Miki .... on this card. (not write)

e The students .... to see the fireworks. (go)

f They .... any food. (not buy)

g I think the show .... (begin)

h All the offices .... work early today. (stop)

i We .... an excellent band for our party. (find)

j .... José .... invitations to all his friends? (send)

2 Shusha is preparing for a party. Look at her list and write sentences about what she's already done and what she hasn't done yet.

> a make a list of all my friends ✓
> b phone them ✗
> c decide where to have the party ✓
> d hire a disco ✗
> e plan the food ✓
> f order the drinks ✓
> g choose a new dress ✗

a *She's already made a list of all her friends.*

b *She hasn't phoned them yet.*

c ....

d ....

e ....

f ....

g ....

3 Complete the sentences. Use *just* + the present perfect of the verb in brackets.

a Angie: Can I use Rita's bicycle?
Gilda: Sorry, but you can't. *She's just gone* out on it. (she/go)

b Bill: Can you give me a lift to the city centre?
Dad: No, I can't. .... the car to the garage. (I/take)

c Harry: Would your girlfriend like some sandwiches?
Kenneth: I don't think so. .... a big lunch. (she/have)

d Selim: Do the students have any plans for the end of term?
Carlo: Yes, ... a table at a restaurant. (they/book)

e Velma: You're very happy this afternoon.
Harriet: I am! .... my driving test. (I/pass)

f Mark: Does your brother want to come clubbing with us?
Alex: Thanks, but .... a new computer game and he wants to try it. (he/buy)

↘ GF page 208

Vocabulary

4 Use the words on the balloons to make expressions
we use on special days.

Happy birthday

a nice weekend
done
good
a good journey
anniversary
enjoy
have
happy
have
birthday
your meal
well
luck
happy

5 Match each email to one of the words in the box.

| apologise | ~~ask~~ | describe | explain | invite | suggest | thank |

a Why has Becca bought a new bikini?

ask

b The room is in a terrible mess because we had a party last night.

c Would you like to have a coffee with me?

d The little girls wore white and carried flowers.

e We've really enjoyed our day. Thank you for inviting us.

f You should arrive at the airport three hours before your flight.

g I'm so sorry, I've lost your dictionary.

Exam skills

Writing Part 2

Your English friend called Gareth has invited you to a barbecue next Sunday but you can't go.

Write an email to Gareth. In your email, you should

- explain why you can't go
- describe a different plan
- ask him if he agrees

Write 35–45 words.

Dear Gareth

How do you feel?

Grammar

1 Simon's parents went away for a week and he stayed at home. They are coming home tomorrow and Simon has some problems. Read the email he sent to his sister, Beth.

○ ○ ○

Dear Beth

Mum and Dad are coming home tomorrow morning and I need to be ready for them. I drove the car into the front fence last week and I broke a headlight. I also used all the petrol. On Monday I played basketball in the dining room and I broke a lamp. On Tuesday I practised my electric guitar and the neighbours complained. On Wednesday I invited ten friends over for a meal and they ate all the food in the freezer. Then yesterday I had a party but everything was OK after that. Please reply soon.
Simon

Beth writes an email back to Simon. Write the advice she gives him using *should, shouldn't, had better* or *Why don't you*. Use some of the ideas in the list below.

repair the fence
ask the neighbours to help
take the car to the garage
buy some more petrol
buy a new lamp
play basketball in the garden next time
apologise to the neighbours for the noise
buy some more food
tell Mum and Dad about the party
stay in the house alone again
have another party

○ ○ ○

Dear Simon
This is what you should do:
You should repair the fence. Why don't you ask the neighbours to help?

.

Love,
Beth

---

2 Complete the short answers.

a 'Does your father work in a shop?'
   'Yes, _he does_ .'
b 'Did you come by bus?'
   'No, ...'
c 'Has the supermarket got a café?'
   'Yes, ...'
d 'Have you got a headache?'
   'No, ...'
e 'Does Lucia live near here?'
   'Yes, ...'
f 'Do we need a visa?'
   'No, ...'
g 'Were your parents angry with you?'
   'Yes, ...'
h 'Did you like the film?'
   'Yes, ...'
i 'Has Simon got a sister?'
   'No, ...'
j 'Has Julia arrived home?'
   'No, ...'

↘ GF page 208

Pronunciation

3 Which words below contain the sound /e/ as in *help* and which words contain the sound /eɪ/ as in *play*? Put them into the correct column.

| always bread break breakfast came |
| fell friend help said sale say train |

/e/ help	/eɪ/ play
	always

Vocabulary

4 Make sentences about these people. What is wrong with them?

a Olga has got a red nose and a sore throat.
  Olga *'s got a cold.*

b Elliot feels hot and cold.
  Elliot's got ....

c Sam ate a large meal and then played basketball for two hours.
  Sam feels ....

d Tom is taking an aspirin. He needs to go to the dentist.
  Tom's got ....

e Katja walked 30 kilometres yesterday.
  Katja's feet ....

f John's son is learning to play the drums. John is sitting in the same room.
  John's got ....

g Kate carried home two heavy bags of shopping yesterday.
  Kate's arms ....

h Gianni shut his finger in the door.
  Gianni's got a ....

i Jessica takes cough mixture every four hours.
  Jessica's got ....

Exam skills

Reading Part 4

Read the text and answer the questions below.

For each question, mark the correct letter A, B, C or D.

> Last Saturday I came to your shop to buy some jazz CDs. I came away with none of them. The last time I came to your shop was two years ago and you sold every kind of music. Now you sell exactly the same as all the other shops – only pop music. Why don't you sell jazz? There is nowhere in this town you can buy a jazz CD. The sales assistants are pleasant and helpful and I asked them why you sell just pop music and DVDs. They didn't know. The shop was nearly empty, so maybe you should ask the customers what they want to buy.

1 What is the writer trying to do?
  A complain about something
  B apologise about something
  C advertise something
  D sell something

2 Why is the writer angry?
  A The sales assistants were rude.
  B He could not buy what he wanted.
  C The shop sold only CDs.
  D He went to the wrong shop.

3 How is the shop different from two years ago?
  A It is busier.
  B It doesn't have enough staff.
  C It is smaller.
  D It doesn't sell jazz CDs.

5 Do this crossword.

Across

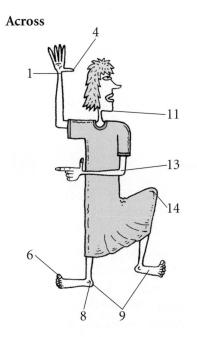

Down

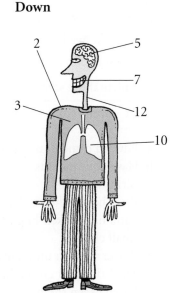

I look forward to hearing from you

Grammar

1   Five of these sentences have a mistake in them. Find the mistakes and correct them. If there is no mistake, write *correct*.

a   ~~I've arrived~~ here three days ago.   *I arrived*

b   Did you have a good time in London?

c   I didn't eat anything since midday.

d   They've started their course in September.

e   Have these letters been here since yesterday?

f   The other students have left half an hour ago.

g   Did you live here all your life?

h   The school has opened in 1990.

2   Complete these sentences with the words in the box.

> ago   ever   for   ~~in~~   since   yet

a   Edward came to my school *in* 2009.

b   Have your parents .... been to Birmingham?

c   Petra has studied in Japan .... six months.

d   Sunil has spoken English .... he was a small child.

e   Xavier went to university a year ....

f   The bride and groom have arrived, but we haven't seen them ....

3   Complete these sentences with either *been* or *gone*.

a   I've *been* .... to the city centre three times this week. I'm not going again.

b   Nika's .... to bed. She's catching an early flight tomorrow.

c   Have you ever .... to Lisbon?

d   I've never .... anywhere as beautiful as Florence. I love it.

e   Jan isn't in college this week. He's .... to visit his grandparents.

f   I can't find anyone in the office. Where have they all .... ?

g   You should talk to Martin about travelling in Mexico. He's .... there five times.

↘ GF page 208

⟲ Corpus spot

4   Here are some sentences by PET students. Correct the mistakes in the verbs.

a   She buyed a lot of presents.

b   The policeman catched the thief.

c   You have choosen a good school.

d   We drinked coffee and talked.

e   My father gived me this watch.

f   I haven't wroten an answer to your letter.

Pronunciation

5 Read these sentences. Mark the words ending in /s/ (as in *books*), /z/ (as in *schools*) or /ɪz/ (as in *glasses*) in different ways, then put them into the correct column.

a There aren't any clean dish<u>es</u>, but there are some cup⑤ and mug<u>s</u>.
b The tram passes our school, but the buses don't.
c She catches the early train on Mondays.
d My brother's friend keeps snakes in the bedroom.
e The weather changes quickly in the mountains.
f When my sister sings, the dog goes out of the room.

books /S/	schools /Z/	glasses /ɪZ/
cups	mugs	dishes

Vocabulary

6 Complete this email. Fill each space with one word beginning with the letter given.

○ ○ ○   ⌒

🚫 ⤺ ⤺ ➡ 🖨
Delete Reply Reply All Forward Print

Dear Mr Molina,

Thank you for your email. We have (**a**) r *eserved* a place for you and your (**b**) f_____ on our summer course. I am sending you an (**c**) a_____ form. Please send it back as soon as possible, with your (**d**) s_____ at the bottom.
(**e**) U_____ there are no rooms free in our student (**f**) h_____ at the time you plan to (**g**) a_____ the school. We can find you (**h**) a_____ with a family. If you would like us to arrange this, please email me the time and date of your (**i**) a_____ .
Yours (**j**) s_____ ,

K. Lewis

Karen Lewis

Office Manager

7 Add the missing vowels to these expressions, then fit them into the spaces in the crossword.

l .o. v .e.
y _ _ rs
l _ v _   fr _ m
_ ll   th _   b _ st
y _ _ rs   s _ nc _ r _ ly
w _ th   b _ st   w _ sh _ s

Facts and figures

Grammar

1 Every year the town of Westville has a festival. Read these sentences about the preparations and put the verbs into the present passive.

a The streets *are decorated* .
(decorate)

b The town ....
(clean)

c The posters ....
(print)

d Important people ....
(invite)

e Special clothes .... for the children.
(make)

f The music ....
(choose)

g The dances .... in the schools.
(practise)

h Cars .... from going into the centre.
(stop)

2 Write sentences about these things, places or people. Use one adjective from the box for each sentence.

expensive	far	good	heavy	hot	large
old	~~tall~~				

a Maxime is 1.78 m tall; Sergio is 1.60 m tall; Adam is 1.72 m tall.
Maxime is the tallest .

b Maxime weighs 82 kg; Sergio weighs 87 kg; Adam weighs 71 kg.
....

c Maxime is 22 years old; Sergio is 20 years old; Adam is 24 years old.
....

d Lake Victoria is 69.5 km^2; Lake Superior is 82.4 km^2; the Caspian Sea is 424.2 km^2.
....

e Buenos Aires is 11,151 km from Rome; Hong Kong is 9,284 km from Rome; Moscow is 2,376 km from Rome.
....

f Maurice Greene ran 100 m in 9.79 seconds; Donovan Bailey ran 100 m in 9.84 seconds; Marion Jones ran 100 m in 10.65 seconds.
....

g A cup of coffee costs €2.5; a glass of water costs €1.5; a glass of juice costs €3.2.
....

h The average daily temperature in Edinburgh in August is 14.3°C; the average daily temperature in San Francisco in August is 27.6°C; the average daily temperature in Montevideo in August is 11.3°C.
....

↘ GF page 208

Vocabulary

3 Find the nationalities of these people in the wordsearch. The words go in all directions.

William Shakespeare   Nelson Mandela   Leo Tolstoy
Pablo Picasso   Leonardo da Vinci   Pelé
Frédéric Chopin   Mahatma Gandhi

A	X	T	D	E	J	C	E	F	A	Y	R
N	R	U	S	M	N	I	L	D	W	T	H
A	G	S	E	B	B	G	I	S	Q	D	S
I	P	Q	I	R	R	U	L	M	B	F	I
S	O	U	T	H	A	F	R	I	C	A	N
S	L	V	A	W	Z	W	S	I	S	S	A
U	I	L	L	Y	I	Z	P	O	V	H	P
R	S	L	I	Q	L	V	E	N	J	W	S
J	H	I	A	P	I	K	H	H	K	J	O
M	A	P	N	E	A	R	U	T	O	B	C
E	N	X	Y	A	N	A	I	D	N	I	X

Pronunciation

4 Fill in the missing letters – *ch* or *sh* – in sentences a–i. Then put them into the correct column below.

a Can you _c h_ange these dollars into pounds, please?
b The ....eapest way to get to Bristol is by coach.
c Liverpool was famous for ....ip-building.
d I wa........ my hair every day in the ....ower.
e You eat too mu........ sugar.
f We could have ....ips with our chicken.
g Why don't you wat........ this programme with me?
h He's a very ....eerful person.
i My ....oulders hurt because I carried my bags from the station.

/t ʃ/ cheese	/ʃ/ shoe
change	

There are two other words in the sentences with the sound /ʃ/ and two other words with the sound /t ʃ/. Can you find them? Put them into the correct column.

Writing

5 Match the numbers to the words.

385   3,589   3,980   350, 859
~~358~~   38, 509   35, 805

a three hundred and fifty-eight *358*
b three thousand, five hundred and eighty-nine
c thirty-five thousand, eight hundred and five
d three hundred and fifty thousand, eight hundred and fifty-nine
e three hundred and eighty-five
f thirty-eight thousand, five hundred and nine
g three thousand, nine hundred and eighty

Exam skills

Writing Part 1

Read these sentences.
Complete the second sentence so that it means the same as the first. Use no more than three words.

1 The ring I bought was more expensive than the others in the shop.
I bought *the most expensive* ring in the shop.
2 The moon is smaller than the earth.
The moon is not .... as the earth.
3 My brother is smaller than all the other boys in his class.
My brother is the .... in his class.
4 Sailing is less tiring than windsurfing.
Sailing is not .... windsurfing.
5 Children are given a quiz when they arrive at the museum.
The museum .... children a quiz when they arrive.
6 I am driven to college every day by my sister.
My sister .... me to college every day.

A good read

Grammar

1 Yesterday, a group of students visited a museum. Their teacher asked them to be ready at ten o'clock, but everyone was late. Write a sentence about what each person was doing at ten o'clock.

At ten o'clock …

a Amelia / read / love story _Amelia was reading a love story._

b Billy / ride / motorbike ....

c Carla / get / dressed ....

d Danny / eat / breakfast ....

e Erica / look for / her mobile ....

f Freddie / phone / his girlfriend ....

g Glenda / play / her guitar ....

h Hugo / listen / Glenda ....

2 Sandy and Moira are sisters. Their home is in Glasgow in Scotland. Sandy is a high school student there. Moira is staying with cousins in Auckland, New Zealand.
Write sentences with *while* + past continuous about what they were both doing yesterday.

a get up / look at the stars
While Sandy was getting up, Moira was looking at the stars.

b sit in the classroom / dream about Scotland

....

....

c do homework / make breakfast for her cousins

....

....

d sit in the cinema / walk on the beach

....

....

e get ready for bed / sail round the Bay of Islands

....

....

f sleep / watch a rugby match

....

....

↘ GF page 209

Pronunciation

3 Read these sentences. Mark the sounds /uː/ as in *two* and /ʊ/ as in *look* in different ways. Then put the words into the correct column.

a Does the sch<u>oo</u>l serve <u>goo</u>d f<u>oo</u>d?

b I can't pull these boots off.

c He took my blue shoes.

d Put the books in the boot of the car.

e The room was full, so I stood on a stool.

/uː/ two	/ʊ/ look
school	good
food	

Writing

4 Think of a television programme you have seen (it needn't be in English). Write a short review of it for the other people in your class. Write 50–60 words. Try to answer these questions in your review.

- What was the programme called and who was in it?
- Was it part of a series?
- If it was non-fiction, what was it about?
- If it was fiction, where did the story take place? What happened?
- What is your opinion of it?

Vocabulary

5 All the answers to this crossword have something to do with books.

Across

2 The kind of books which are about real facts.
4 Books about exciting events.
5 Any book which tells a long story.
6 Something we don't understand.
9 Not 2 across!
10 This gives someone's opinion about a book (or a film).

Down

1 A book which tells someone's life story.
3 Stories about ghosts and other frightening things.
4 This is a foreign book in your language.
7 Some people are very good at telling these.
8 What poets write.

Exam skills

Writing Part 3

These sentences tell a story, but they are in the wrong order. Read the sentences and put them in the correct order. Then choose a title from the box.

a She was walking towards a busy road.
b 'Well, who did? Because that's why I didn't cross the road,' she said.
c After a few minutes, my mother realised that Agnes wasn't with us.
d My father was looking round the town while my mother was watching Agnes and me on the beach.
e It was very dangerous.
f 'Where's Daddy?' she asked.
g 'No,' said my father and Agnes looked surprised.
h We looked around and we saw her.
i When my father arrived a few minutes later, Agnes asked him, 'Did you call me?'
j When I was six my parents took my little sister, Agnes, and me to the seaside one afternoon.
k Suddenly she stopped and walked back to us.

1 __j__   2 _____   3 _____   4 _____
5 _____   6 _____   7 _____   8 _____
9 _____   10 _____   11 _____

Titles
Happy holidays
An unusual journey
Bad luck
A strange event
Brothers and sisters

13 A place of my own

Grammar

1 Look at the picture and complete the description below, using the words in the box.

above	below
between	~~on~~
on top of	opposite
over	~~in the corner~~
side by side	

This is a picture of an antique shop window. It has a carpet (**a**) ....*on*.......... the floor. There's a round table (**b**) ....*in*........ ..*the corner*.. ,with a kind of box (**c**) .... it. On the wall (**d**) .... it, there's a painting, and (**e**) .... that, on the other wall, there's a pair of mirrors hanging (**f**) .... There's a chair (**g**) .... the mirrors. The chair has a cloth (**h**) .... it. A chest of drawers stands (**i**) .... the chair and the table.

2 Choose the correct verb.

a Is Terry playing in the match today?
He *might*/*must* be. He's wearing his football boots.

b Is Penelope worried about her exam this afternoon?
She *mustn't*/*can't* be. She went clubbing last night!

c Is Leon good at playing the guitar?
He *must*/*could* be. He won an international music prize last year.

d Is Norma allowed to drive her mother's car?
She *must*/*can't* be, because she hasn't got a driving licence.

e Are the children playing a computer game?
They *must*/*could* be. Or perhaps they're doing their homework!

↘ GF page 209

Pronunciation

3 Read these sentences. Mark the sounds /ʒ/ as in *television* and /dʒ/ as in *joke* in different ways. Then put the words into the correct column below.

a I write three pages of revision notes every day.

b There's usually some juice in the fridge.

c Can you join us to look round the college?

d The weather is generally good in August, but not in January.

e We must measure the lounge before we make a decision about furniture.

f What age was John when he made that journey?

/ʒ/ television	/dʒ/ joke
revision	pages

Vocabulary

4 Complete this word tree with the names of furniture you find in the different rooms.

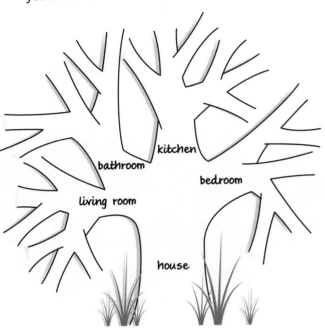

kitchen
bathroom
bedroom
living room
house

5 Write the names of the parts of this house.

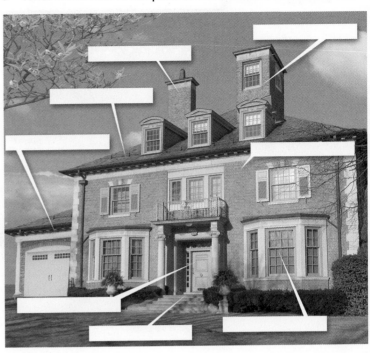

Exam skills

Reading Part 5

Read the text and choose the correct word for each space. For each question, mark the correct letter A, B, C or D.

MY FIRST HOME

When my parents married, they rented a small house and they didn't have a lot of money for furniture. The kitchen had a (1) .... for washing up and a cooker, but that was all. They (2) .... an old table and chairs from the market. They borrowed a sofa which was (3) .... old, but they (4) .... it with modern materials so it was bright and cheerful. Outside, there was a small garden (5) .... the house, but in front of it there was only the road. Luckily the road wasn't busy, so I could cross it to (6) .... the park on the (7) .... side. We lived there (8) .... I was ten and we were very happy. We had to (9) .... house because it was too small when my twin sisters were born. We all (10) .... sad when we left.

	A	B	C	D
1	basin	cupboard	Ⓒ sink	bath
2	bought	sold	became	brought
3	more	also	even	little
4	placed	put	covered	made
5	before	through	by	behind
6	reach	arrive	go	get
7	wrong	opposite	different	facing
8	when	after	until	to
9	move	change	leave	close
10	spent	thought	had	felt

14 What's in fashion?

Daniela

Alma

Grammar

1 Daniela's parents are successful fashion designers and live in a house with fifteen bedrooms. Alma's parents have a small shop selling newspapers and sweets and live in a flat above the shop. Use these ideas:

help in a shop
walk to school
wear designer clothes
go camping for her holiday
have lots of pocket money

travel to school in an expensive car
wear her sister's old clothes
go to a luxury hotel for her holiday
share a bedroom with her sister

Write two sentences with *used to* about what Daniela did when she was a child.

....

....

Write two sentences with *didn't use to* about what Daniela didn't do when she was a child.

....

....

Write two sentences with *used to* about what Alma did when she was a child.

....

....

Write two sentences with *didn't use to* about what Alma didn't do when she was a child.

....

....

2 Complete these sentences with an adjective (+ *enough* if necessary).

a Oliver doesn't like going to parties because he's too *shy* .

b Kyla can't run 1,000 metres because she isn't *fit enough* .

c We can't walk to the station. It's too ....

d Jack can't ride a motorbike yet. He's only 13, so he isn't ....

e We missed the train by two minutes. We were too ....

f I can't see the stars because it isn't ....

g I can never hear what Sian says because her voice isn't ....

h I can't afford to take a taxi. They're too ....

i I can't reach the top shelf because I'm too ....

j It isn't snowing today because it isn't ....

3 Add the adjectives in brackets to the sentences below. Put them in the correct order.

a We have a lot of (wooden / old / horrible) furniture in our flat.
We have a lot of horrible, old wooden furniture in our flat.

b My brother loves playing (rock / loud) music.

....

c My sister gave me some (silver / lovely / long) earrings.

....

d The shop was full of (plastic / expensive) toys.

....

e I wore my (blue / cotton / new) dress to the party.

....

f My mother has (black / short) hair.

....

↘ GF page 209

Vocabulary

4 You are writing a report for a fashion magazine. Write about what these models are wearing.

The woman is wearing black trousers ....

....

....

....

....

The man is wearing ....

....

....

....

....

....

5 There are eleven colours in this wordsearch. Can you find them? They go in all directions.

T	P	M	K	L	E	O	Y	M
P	B	U	M	G	W	R	E	D
N	W	O	R	B	O	A	U	H
U	S	E	J	P	L	N	L	B
B	Y	W	Y	O	L	G	B	J
T	W	H	I	T	E	E	K	P
P	A	L	R	I	Y	O	F	I
L	N	E	E	R	G	S	Z	N
K	C	A	L	B	A	R	I	K

Pronunciation

6 Underline the letters which make the sound /f/.

a My <u>f</u>avourite subject is geogra<u>ph</u>y but I also like <u>ph</u>ysics.

b The photographer was on the phone when the film star came through the door, so he missed her.

c Someone was holding a light but we weren't near enough to see who it was.

d They laughed at the sight of the baby elephant playing.

e The sea was very rough and we were frightened.

🔽 **Corpus spot**

7 Here are some sentences by PET students. Correct the mistakes.

a My coat has a nice green colour.

b There was a long queue because it was a fashion restaurant.

c My brother always wears short and a T shirt.

d I don't wear the same cloths every day.

e My black trouser is dirty.

f She's wearing blue dress.

15 Risk!

Grammar

1 Choose the correct verb.

a Doctors *can* / <u>*have to*</u> train for several years before they are qualified.

b Lorries *mustn't* / *don't have to* use this route because it's too narrow.

c You *can't* / *don't have to* stop at the shop on your way here because I've already bought some food.

d Students *can* / *have to* borrow up to twelve books from the library.

e Peter has already heard the news so you *mustn't* / *don't have to* phone him.

f You *can't* / *don't have to* phone your friend in Moscow because it costs too much.

g Guests *can* / *have to* pay their hotel bills by credit card if they prefer.

h You *can* / *must* reply to Anna's email today because she's going away tomorrow.

i I *can* / *have to* ask my parents' permission before I borrow their car.

j You *can't* / *don't have to* watch a DVD now because I'm watching the news.

2 Jack is working at a summer activity camp for children. He is telling Laura about the rules. Read part of the handbook for workers and complete the conversation using *can* / *can't* / *have to* / *don't have to*.

HANDBOOK FOR WORKERS

REMEMBER!

☞ **Get up by 6.30 am.**

☞ **Make breakfast for children.**

☞ **Take the register after breakfast.**

☞ **Use the pool any time except when there are lessons.**

☞ **Food and accommodation in staff hostel free!**

☞ **No food in rooms.**

☞ **No parties.**

☞ **Free time in evening.**

☞ **Bus to town every half hour in the evening.**

☞ **Keep rooms clean and tidy.**

Jack: Hi, Laura. Welcome to the camp. Have you found your room?

Laura: Yes. It's nice. I haven't paid for it yet. I'm glad we (**a**) <u>*don't have to*</u> share the hostel with the children.

Jack: We (**b**) .... pay for food or accommodation but we (**c**) .... clean our rooms. We eat all our meals in the canteen. We (**d**) .... keep food in our rooms.

Laura: So do we spend every day with the children?

Jack: Yes, we (**e**) .... get up by 6.30 am and then we (**f**) .... make breakfast for the children. After that we (**g**) .... take the register before the activities begin.

Laura: What about free time?

Jack: We (**h**) .... use the pool any time except when there are lessons. In the evening we (**i**) .... work, so we (**j**) .... take the bus to town if we want. But we (**k**) .... have parties in the hostel.

3 Each of these sentences has an adjective in it. In some of the sentences you need to change the adjective into an adverb. Write the correct adverb. Four of the sentences are correct.

a My grandfather drives very ~~slow~~. *slowly*

b My friend helped me move the TV because it was very heavy. *correct*

c We left the room quiet because we didn't want to wake the baby up.

d The weather was perfect yesterday.

e I opened the envelope nervous.

f The teacher spoke angry to the students.

g My new bed is really comfortable.

h I opened my eyes sleepy when I heard the alarm.

i We waited miserable at the bus stop in the rain.

j Don't be frightened. I will help you.

k Luca smiled happy when he heard the news.

 GF page 210

Vocabulary

4 Put a suitable verb with *get* in each space.

When I go rock-climbing I always **(a)** *get up* early. I catch the first bus to the mountains because I like to **(b)** .... the climb before it's too hot. I always start to feel nervous when I **(c)** .... the bus and wonder how I will **(d)** .... Sometimes I go with a friend but I always choose someone I **(e)** .... and can trust.

Pronunciation

5 How do we pronounce the letters *ou*? Which word is the odd one out in each list?

a double   couple   <u>your</u>   rough
b house   shout   round   touch
c thought   bought   enough   ought
d nervous   young   colour   flavour
e dangerous   loud   about   mouth

Exam skills

Reading Part 1

Look at these signs.
What do they say?
Mark the correct letter A, B or C.

1

PHOTOGRAPHY DARKROOM

DO NOT ENTER WHEN RED LIGHT IS ON

A You can go in when you see the red light.
B When the red light is off you can go in.
C You must not turn the light on when you enter this room.

2

BUS DRIVER ONLY SELLS SINGLE TICKETS FOR TODAY

WEEKLY TICKETS AVAILABLE AT TICKET OFFICE

A You can't buy a weekly ticket in advance.
B You can buy a ticket for one journey from the bus driver.
C You can only buy a weekly ticket on this bus.

Grammar

1 Make six sensible sentences by matching these halves.

1 I'm going to buy a motorbike   **a** when I go clubbing.
2 I'm going to save   **b** after I leave school.
3 I'm going to phone my boyfriend   **c** until I have enough money for a holiday.
4 I'm going to wear my new T-shirt   **d** when I get a motorbike.
5 I'm going to dance   **e** until I feel tired.
6 I'm going to buy some leather jeans   **f** after I get home from school.

2 Complete these conversations, using one word in each space.

Conversation 1

I'm going to (**a**) _run_ a marathon! Would you like to (**b**) _____ me?

I'm (**c**) _____ I can't. Another time (**d**) _____ .

Conversation 2

I'm going to go karting this afternoon. Would you like to (**e**) _____ with me?

Oh sorry, I'm going to (**f**) _____ busy then.

(**g**) _____ about another time?

Er ...

Conversation 3

We're going to get married. Do you (**h**) _____ to be our bridesmaid?

Thank you for (**i**) _____ me. I'd really (**j**) _____ that.

3 Put the verbs in this magazine interview into the correct form: *going to* or present simple.

`↘ GF page 210`

Artist J.C. O'Reilly has just had a very successful one-woman exhibition at a top London gallery. Our reporter Paul Amery talked to her.

Paul Congratulations on a very successful exhibition. **What are your plans now?**

J.C. Well, first (**a**) _I'm going to tidy_ (I / tidy) my studio.

Paul **It looks OK to me.**

J.C. It's a terrible mess. I haven't cleaned up for months because I've been so busy, but (**b**) _____ (I / throw away) all the rubbish and (**c**) _____ (I / wash) the walls!

Paul **And after that?**

J.C. Then (**d**) _____ (I / take) a short trip to South America with a friend.

Paul (**e**) _____ **(you / paint) any pictures there?**

J.C. No, (**f**) _____ (I / not / work) until (**g**) _____ (we / come) home. But I know (**h**) _____ (I / get) ideas for new pictures when (**i**) _____ (I / see) all the fantastic mountains and forests.

Paul (**j**) _____ **(you / have) another exhibition soon?**

J.C. I hope so, but (**k**) _____ (I / not / decide) anything before (**l**) _____ (we / go away).

Paul **I can understand that. Well, thank you, J.C., for talking to me. And I look forward to seeing your new work.**

J.C. Thank you.

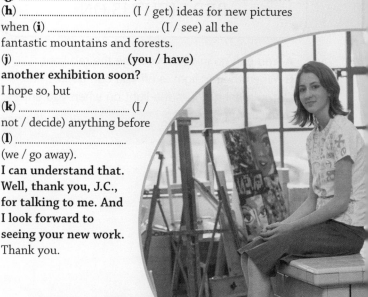

Writing

4 Say the time on these clocks aloud, then write each one in words.

  a

  b

 c

 d

 half past seven

 e

f

 g

h

Vocabulary

5 There are nine words from Unit 16 in this wordsearch. Can you find them? They go in all directions.

K	N	O	C	K	D	Z	W	E	L	Q	F
T	B	E	W	B	I	A	B	E	P	E	R
C	F	G	J	O	W	L	A	Q	R	J	E
O	L	Q	N	Z	N	P	L	A	E	M	T
R	U	B	B	I	S	H	S	V	L	A	U
G	J	W	C	M	B	O	T	E	A	R	P
A	A	N	F	S	T	B	U	K	X	S	M
N	E	R	S	F	S	Q	U	S	T	H	O
I	D	E	T	N	E	C	S	L	X	A	C
S	M	R	J	E	Y	O	G	E	C	A	B
E	B	R	K	N	R	O	Z	J	I	F	A
D	A	V	V	D	S	L	P	R	I	B	K

Exam skills

Writing Part 1

Here are some sentences about a new flat.
For each question, complete the second sentence so that it means the same as the first. Use no more than three words.

1 I have never lived in a flat before.
   This is the first time I *have ever lived* in a flat.

2 My new flat is near the station.
   My new flat is not .... the station.

3 The flat is bigger than my old one.
   The flat is not .... my old one.

4 I moved into this flat two weeks ago.
   I .... in this flat for two weeks.

5 The flat has two bedrooms.
   There .... two bedrooms in the flat.

6 From my window, I have a lovely view.
   From my window, the view .... lovely.

7 From this flat, my journey to work is very short.
   I get to work very .... from this flat.

Next week's episode

Grammar

1 Put the verbs into the correct tense: *will* future or present simple.

International Language College,
High Street, Gretton

Information for new students

TRAVEL

Arrival by train

When **(a)** *you arrive* .... (you / arrive) at Gretton, **(b)** *we will meet* ...... (we / meet) you at the station.

Arrival by bus

Show the driver this brochure and **(c)** .... (he / stop) at the school.

Arrival by car

Please go to your accommodation and park there. **(d)** .... (Your family / look after) you until **(e)** .... (you / come) to school to begin classes. Please remember that **(f)** .... (there / not / be) space for you to park at the school.

ACCOMMODATION

Family stay

(g) .... (We / send) you the address when **(h)** .... (we / receive) your application form. Please phone or write to the family. They need to know the answers to these questions:

What date and time **(i)** .... (you / arrive) in Gretton?

How **(j)** .... (you / travel)?

(k) .... (you / need) a parking space for a car?

Hostel

Please write to our accommodation officer. She needs to know the answers to these questions:

How many weeks **(l)** .... (you / stay) at the hostel?

(m) .... (you / bring) a car?

Would you like an evening meal at the hostel after **(n)** .... (you / arrive)?

2 Finish these sentences using the correct form of *to have something done*.

a Emma went to the hairdresser's yesterday and he cut her hair.
Yesterday Emma *had her hair cut* .

b A friend took Cristina's photo by the fountain.
Cristina .... by the fountain.

c My parents paid a builder to build a garage for them.
My parents ....

d In England, supermarkets deliver the shopping to some people.
In England, some people ....

e When I am rich, I will employ a chef to cook all my meals.
When I am rich, I ....

f Our car was making a strange noise but the mechanic repaired it last week.
We .... last week.

3 Fill the spaces with *anyone, someone, no one* or *everyone*.

a I knocked on the door three times but
no one answered.

b Does .... know the answer to this question?

c I thought .... was following me but when I turned round I couldn't see ....

d .... in my family likes sport, so we often watch matches together.

e I've brought the wrong clothes because .... warned me about the weather.

f I don't know .... who enjoys doing housework.

↘ **GF page 210**

Pronunciation

4 Read these sentences and mark the sounds /ɑ:/ as in *car*, /ɔ:/ as in *saw* or /ɜ:/ as in *hurt* in different ways. Put the words into the correct column below.

a Will Paul ever return to the farm?

b I've been all round the world, but I haven't visited Berlin.

c We can't park here, we'll make a mark on the lawn.

d She's bought an awful card showing a heart and some flowers.

e We aren't poor, because we work hard.

f Would you like half of this burger, or can you eat more?

g He laughed when he saw the bird in the hall.

h They've caught the third burglar.

/ɑ:/ car	/ɔ:/ saw	/ɜ:/ hurt
farm	Paul	return

Vocabulary

5 Answer the clues to find the word down the middle of this puzzle. All the words are in Unit 17 Listening.

1 A place where students study.

2 How much you think something is worth.

3 To use something with another person.

4 People who live in the same flat.

5 To use something which belongs to someone else.

6 You don't want to do this to your friend's car, do you?

7 An event which may cause 6 to happen to something.

8 Argument.

9 The money you pay to 1 for your classes.

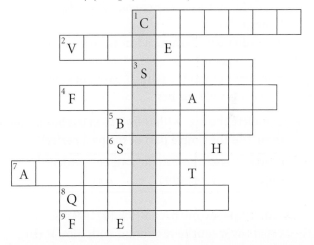

Grammar

1 Choose the correct form of the verbs.

a I hadn't ever been on a long flight until I *flew* / *had flown* to California last year.

b Louisa *changed* / *had changed* her hairstyle, so I didn't recognise her at first.

c I was very tired when I got to the hotel, so I *went* / *had gone* to sleep.

d The café was empty because everyone *went* / *had gone* home.

e I gave the book to my friend when I *read* / *had read* it.

f When I received the email, I *sent* / *had sent* a reply immediately.

g I didn't have Karen's address, so I *phoned* / *had phoned* her to get it.

h When I got to the party, I gave Lucy the present I *bought* / *had bought* for her.

2 Complete the text with the verbs in the box in the correct form. Use the simple past or the past perfect.

> arrive ~~ask~~ be invite open order
> promise remember see sing

Last Thursday my friend Jack (**a**) ...*asked*........................... me to eat at my favourite restaurant with him. It (**b**) .... my birthday and Jack (**c**) ....
(never) it before so I was surprised.
I (**d**) .... at the restaurant half an hour late because a few days before I (**e**) .... to help a friend mend his car and it took a long time. When I
(**f**) .... the restaurant door, I
(**g**) .... twenty friends at the table. Jack
(**h**) .... them all and they (**i**) ....
.... (already) my favourite dinner. At the end of the meal they (**j**) .... 'Happy Birthday'.

↘ GF page 210

Vocabulary

3 Make some words which end in *-tion*. Use the letters in the diagram. Here are some clues to help you.

a You look at this in a museum.
...*exhibition*...........

b You go to this desk when you arrive at a hotel. ....

c You will take this when you finish your course. ....

d You get this at school. ....

e You ask for this when you don't know about something. ....

f This comes before an answer.
....

g You ask 'Which ... is the city centre?' when you are lost. ....

h You go here to catch a train.
....

i This type of book has a story in it.
....

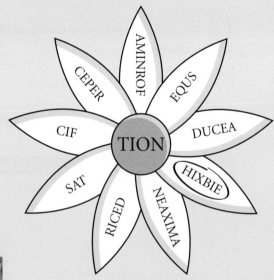

Pronunciation

4 Which of these words have the sound /ə/ in the last syllable (as in *camera, letter, important*)?
Put a tick or a cross.

actor ✓   aeroplane   answer   appointment   artist
different   doctor   magazine   position   shoulder
story ✗   teacher   tourist   translation   visitor

Exam skills

Reading Part 2

The people below (1–5) all want to see a film.
Below are eight film reviews.
Decide which film (A–H) would be the most suitable for the following people.
Mark the correct letter (A–H).

1 Eleni enjoys comedies with a happy ending.
2 Sofia likes adventure films which are exciting from beginning to end.
3 Matteo would like to see a historical film which has a good story.
4 Robert likes watching science fiction films. He likes both cartoons and films with real actors.
5 Julia would like to see a love story with some famous actors. She enjoys films which contain singing and dancing.

A
The Girl in Black is a story about something that happened 400 years ago. Two young people meet and fall in love but the young man has to go away to fight in a war. The story starts well but then nothing really happens.

B
The Circle of Life is a film everyone should see if they want to go home feeling cheerful. I couldn't stop laughing. There is one sad part in the middle but everything is all right in the end. Jules Verity, the star, normally sings and dances in films so this is a change for him.

C
The Last Time stars Jennifer Nolan and Peter O'Bride. We follow their lives separately for the first half of the film until they meet and fall in love. I hadn't realised that it was a musical – this is the first time these well-known actors have appeared in one.

D
The clothes the actors wear in *Cramer Place* are lovely. It is a true story which takes place in the nineteenth century in an old house. It is actually difficult to believe this really happened and I found it impossible to guess the ending – you just have to wait and see. The acting is wonderful.

E
The Blue Country is an action film with a difference because it is also funny (until the end when everyone dies). Most of the action actually comes at the end and I did find the first half a little boring.

F
I hadn't heard of any of the actors in *The Lost Journey* but I'm sure we'll see them again. The film takes place on a small planet in the future. It is rather difficult to believe but it has a good story and is well acted. I loved the ending, which I hadn't expected.

G
The Tree is a cartoon film which contains some wonderful songs. Most of the voices are done by very famous actors and I enjoyed trying to decide who they were. The action takes place in a forest and small children might be frightened by this.

H
The Path to Nowhere is the latest in a series of films starring Des Riley and Tom Carver. It starts with a car chase, there is plenty of action in the middle and it finishes with a helicopter following the two men as they try to escape in a boat. I couldn't wait to discover what happened.

Grammar

1 Match the two halves of these sentences.

1 I'm feeling better, so I hope   *h*
2 It was cold and dark, so I decided
3 I enjoy dancing, so I would like
4 We're going swimming, so you need
5 I haven't seen the film, so I don't mind
6 Cath is really good at
7 I'm looking forward
8 I'm fed up with

a learning new languages.
b waiting for the bus.
c to learn the samba.
d coming with you.
e to catch the train home.
f to seeing you again.
g to bring a towel.
h to come to school tomorrow.

2 Choose *make* or *let* and put the verb in its correct form.

a My mum *makes* me tidy my bedroom on Saturday afternoons.
b My cousin is an actor and sometimes he .... me go backstage to meet the other actors.
c Because I was late for work on Friday, my boss .... me work an extra half-hour at the end of the day.
d The week before the last match, the football manager .... the team practise for six hours every day and he (not) .... them go out in the evenings.
e I (never) .... you borrow my CDs again because you don't take care of them.
f When I was ten years old, my father .... me go to bed at 8.30 on a weekday but he .... me stay up later at the weekend.
g My friend .... me use her phone yesterday because I'd left mine at home.
h The policeman stopped me but luckily he (not) .... me pay a fine.

⬊ GF page 211

Vocabulary

3 Do this crossword.

Across

1 My mother's brother.
6 I call my mother this.
7 My husband's sister.
9 I call my father this.
11 My father's wife (not my mother).
12 My child (female).

Down

2 My brother's son.
3 I am his wife.
4 My aunt's child.
5 My father's father.
8 My child (male).
10 My mother's brother's wife.

Pronunciation

4 Read these words aloud. In which words is *th* pronounced /θ/ as in *thin* and in which words is *th* pronounced /ð/ as in *then*? Underline the odd one out in each group.

a <u>leather</u>   teeth   third   thought
b brother   thriller   their   them
c through   that   thin   bath
d throat   thief   together   thanks

Exam skills

Reading Part 3

Read this text and decide if the sentences 1–6 are correct or incorrect.
If a sentence is correct, write **A**.
If it is incorrect, write **B**.

1 Stella has three sisters. *B*
2 Stella's mother was a photographer.
3 Stella met Naomi Campbell and Kate Moss for the first time at her fashion show in 1995.
4 Everyone was surprised when Stella McCartney was on the front page of the newspapers.
5 Stella had jobs in fashion before she left college.
6 Stella thinks about the kinds of clothes famous models like to wear when she is designing.

Stella McCartney was born in 1972, the daughter of pop star Sir Paul McCartney. She is the youngest of three sisters. One sister is a potter and the other sister does the same job as their mother used to do – she works as a photographer. Stella's brother, James, is a musician. Stella first hit the newspaper headlines in 1995 when she graduated in fashion design from art college. At her final show, her clothes were modelled by her friends, Naomi Campbell and Kate Moss, both well-known models. Unsurprisingly, the student show became front-page news around the world. Stella hadn't been in the news before as a fashion designer but she had spent time working in the fashion world since she was fifteen. In March 1997, Stella went to work for the fashion house Chloe. People said the famous fashion house had given her the job because of her surname and her famous parents but Stella soon showed how good she was. She designs clothes which she would like to wear herself, although she's not a model, and many famous models and actors choose to wear them. In 2001 Stella started her own fashion house and has since opened stores around the world and won many prizes.

So you think you've got talent?

Grammar

1 Make adverbs from the adjectives in the box and use them to make sentences about these people.

~~bad~~   good   healthy   quick   quiet   slow

a Claudia got 100% in the violin exam; Felipe got 98%; Carlos got 90%.
Carlos played *the worst.*

b Irene eats burgers and chips every day; Katharine eats salad and fish every day.
Katharine eats more .... than Irene.

c Margarita types 25 words a minute; Sergio types 40 words a minute; Francesca types 60 words a minute.
Francesca types the ....

d Julia drives at 50 km per hour; Adam drives at 80 km per hour; Graham drives at 65 km per hour.
Julia drives the ....

e Alan speaks French like a Frenchman; Megan is learning French.
Alan speaks French .... than Megan.

f I can hear what Bob says; I can't hear what William says.
Bob speaks .... than William.

2 Join the two sentences with *so* or *such*.

a We arrived late. I missed the plane.
We arrived so late that we missed the plane.

b There was a long queue. I decided to come back later.
There was such a long queue that I decided to come back later.

c The film was boring. I switched the TV off.
....

d My mum drives quickly. She frightens me.
....

e She has long hair. It takes hours to dry.
....

f It was cold. I wore two pairs of socks.
....

g *Far Planet* is a good film. I want to see it again.
....

h The food was awful. I couldn't eat it.
....

i We have an old car. It often breaks down.
....

j This coffee is strong. I can't drink it.
....

3 Complete the text with the words in the box. Use some of them twice.

although   as soon as   because
but   either   or   so

When I was about fourteen, I wanted to be (**a**) *either* .... a pop singer (**b**) .... a dancer. My parents thought that was a bad idea (**c**) .... it's very difficult to get work as a singer (**d**) .... a dancer. They wanted me to study law (**e**) .... I wasn't really interested in working as a lawyer. They persuaded me, and I studied law at university. (**f**) .... I left university, I found a job as a lawyer. After a few years I got bored with it, (**g**) .... I decided to do something different. (**h**) .... it was very badly paid, I took a job with a record company. (**i**) .... I started there I realised I'd made the wrong decision. The job wasn't exciting at all, (**j**) .... I found another job as a lawyer and I sing in a club in the evenings.

⬎ GF page 211

Pronunciation and spelling

4 Choose the correct word to complete each sentence.

there/their

a What's ...*their*... address?

b How many students are .... in the college?

c I saw Olga at the party but Misha wasn't ....

hear/here

d Did you .... the news about Frankie?

e Sorry, Ed isn't .... at the moment.

f Turn the TV up. I can't .... what they're saying.

Exam skills

Writing Part 1

Here are some sentences about a musical show.

For each question, complete the second sentence so that it means the same as the first. Use no more than three words.

1 Tickets are sold in the box office until 8 pm.
The box office ...*sells*... tickets until 8 pm.

2 There was such a tall man in front of me that I couldn't see very well.
The man in front of me was .... that I couldn't see very well.

3 The band played too softly, so it was difficult to hear the music.
The band didn't play .... , so it was difficult to hear the music.

4 Some of the performers were very good dancers indeed.
Some of the performers danced very .... indeed.

5 My favourite part was the last song.
The part I liked .... was the last song.

6 We should come to musicals more often.
We ought .... to musicals more often.

Writing Part 3

This is part of a letter you receive from an English penfriend called Alex.

> In your next letter, tell me all about the music you and your family like.

Lucas wrote this answer. Read his answer and then fill the spaces with your own words to write your own answer.

Dear Alex
I like listening to different kinds of music. My favourite is garage music but I also like rock. My sisters like hip-hop or pop music and my parents prefer rock and classical music. We all like watching talent shows on TV. I play music on my laptop in my bedroom. I like listening to music when I'm relaxing and when I'm doing my homework. I don't really like dancing but my sisters do. They enjoy going to nightclubs. I play the guitar and I'd like to play the guitar in a band.
Write back soon.
Lucas

I like listening to .... My favourite is .... but I also like .... My sister(s)/brother(s)/ cousins/friends like .... and my parents/grandparents prefer .... We all like / None of us like .... I play music .... I like listening to music when .... I (don't) like dancing and/but .... I (don't) play .... and/but I'd like to play ....

Grammar

1 What did these people say?

a The customer asked the shop assistant to show him some jackets.
He said, '*Please show me* .... some jackets.'

b The businesswoman told the visitors to leave her office immediately.
She said, '*Leave my office* .... immediately.'

c I asked my brother not to tell anyone.
I said, '.................. anyone.'

d The millionaire told his secretary to answer all his letters.
He said, '.................. all my letters.'

e The actress told her driver not to open the car door.
She said, '.................. the car door.'

f The photographer asked the sports star to wave to the crowd.
He said, '.................. to the crowd.'

g The hairdresser asked her friends not to phone her at work.
She said, '.................. at work.'

2 Report these requests and commands.

a She said, 'Please lend me some money, Clive.'
She asked *Clive to lend her some money* .

b 'Don't put anything on my desk, Sonia,' said Tristan.
Tristan told Sonia *not to put anything on his desk* .

c 'Can you phone the bank, please, Mrs Ware?' said the salesman.
The salesman asked Mrs Ware ....

d 'Please don't touch my motorbike, Alan,' I said.
I asked ....

e The manager said, 'Don't go into my office, Patrick.'
The manager told ....

f 'Please tidy all the shelves, Heidi,' said Annette.
Annette ....

g 'Alex, give me my jacket,' said Ivan.
Ivan ....

↘ GF page 212

3 Write some true sentences about people you know, using some of these beginnings.

One of my aunts *has a motorbike.*
One of my classmates ....
A neighbour of mine ....
One of my cousins ....
A colleague of mine ....
One of my brothers/sisters ....
A friend of mine ....
One of my favourite singers ....

4 Write the expressions we use when we make and answer phone calls.

a Say who you are.
This is Molly.
....

b Ask to speak to Mr Jonas.
....

c Ask for the caller's name.
....

d Ask the caller to wait.
....

e Tell a caller that Mr Jonas cannot speak to them this evening.
....

f Ask a caller to phone again at another time.
....

↘ Corpus spot ◉

5 Three of these sentences contain mistakes by PET students. Find them and correct them.

a I texted my friend about the news.
b Please call me at my mobile.
c I need a mobile to phone to my parents.
d They were angry because he didn't switch his phone to silent.
e I rang to the police and told them what happened.
f I asked him to call me back.

Vocabulary

6 Can you find ten words or phrases about phoning in this circle? Use your dictionary to check meanings.

top up
missed call
switch off
hang on
switch on
mobile
text
in tune
hole
equipment
ring
call back
action
shame
solve
check
carry away
hang up
remind
crew

Exam skills

Reading Part 5

Read the text and choose the correct word for each space.
For each question, mark the correct letter **A**, **B**, **C** or **D**.

POCKET MONEY

I was sixteen when I got my (1) .... job. The man who
(2) .... our local supermarket was one of my
(3) .... friends. She (4) .... him that I was
hard-working and needed to (5) .... some money. He gave
me an interview, and after a few questions he told me to start work.
The (6) .... were not good, but I worked every evening
(7) .... twelve weeks and saved enough money for a short
holiday with my friends. I was very (8) .... to be able to
pay for everything I wanted (9) .... of asking my parents
for money. Since that time, I have always (10) .... a job as
well as studying.

1	**A** primary	**(B)** first	**C** one	**D** only
2	**A** held	**B** began	**C** turned	**D** ran
3	**A** mother	**B** mothers	**C** mother's	**D** mothers'
4	**A** told	**B** said	**C** asked	**D** spoke
5	**A** keep	**B** earn	**C** bring	**D** take
6	**A** charges	**B** fees	**C** wages	**D** fares
7	**A** until	**B** of	**C** through	**D** for
8	**A** proud	**B** great	**C** fun	**D** generous
9	**A** against	**B** instead	**C** except	**D** without
10	**A** do	**B** done	**C** doing	**D** did

Strange but true?

Grammar

1 **What did these people say?**

a The girl said she often watched science fiction films.
She said, '*I often watch* .... science fiction films.'

b The engineer said he had checked his car in the morning.
He said, '*I checked my car* .... in the morning.'

c I said I didn't like that kind of story.
I said, '... that kind of story.'

d The pilot said he had already spoken to the airport.
He said, '.. to the airport.'

e The woman said she usually kept her phone in her bag.
She said, '.. bag.'

f The scientist said he hadn't believed the children's stories at first.
He said, '............................... the children's stories at first.'

g The alien said it had seen enough of this planet and it was ready to leave.
It said, '............................... enough of this planet and .... ready to leave.'

2 **Report these statements.**

a He said, 'I always tell the truth.'
He said *he always told* .... the truth.

b 'I didn't feel frightened,' said the boy.
The boy said *he hadn't felt* .... frightened.

c The teacher said, 'I've never heard any strange noises.'
The teacher said .... any strange noises.

d 'I saw a strange light in the garden,' said the policeman.
The policeman said .... a strange light in the garden.

e The soldier said, 'I don't want to hurt anyone.'
The soldier said .... to hurt anyone.

f 'I sometimes watch DVDs with my friends,' said Joanna.
Joanna said .... friends.

g The aliens said, 'We've been here for a long time but no one has known about us.'
The aliens said .... for a long time but no one ....

↘ GF page 212

Pronunciation

3 **Read these sentences. Write the words with silent consonants in them and mark the silent consonants. Practise saying the words.**

a Can you write with your book on your knee?
write knee

b We keep science materials in the cupboard.
....

c Although he's not rich, I think he's honest.
....

d Who bought Thomas a new comb?
....

e I've brought the wrong receipt.
....

f Where's the other half of the cake?
....

g He can't use these scissors because his right wrist is broken.
....

h I answered the email last night.
....

Vocabulary

4 Put the vowels into these words and write the words in the crossword. All the words are in Unit 22.

Across
1 D _ SC
4 P_SS_B_L_TY
6 _XPL_N_T_ _N
7 CH_ST
9 P_RC_NT_G_
11 SP_C_CR_FT
13 T_ _CH
14 B_L_ _V_
15 R_NG
16 _PPR_ _CH

Down
2 C_LL_CT
3 SC_ _NC_
5 S_ _RCH
8 D_C_ _V_
10 TR_CK
12 F_CT_ _N
14 B_TT_N

5 Fill each space with a word from the box.

approve	dislike	disagree	doubt	expect
prefer	~~respect~~			

a I _respect_ people who work hard for their money.

b I .... preparing for a party to cleaning the house after it.

c I don't .... of people texting during meals.

d I .... with most of my friends about modern art.

e I .... whether all my friends will remember my birthday.

f I don't .... my parents and I will ever agree about politics.

g I .... getting up early in the morning.

Exam skills

Writing Part 2

It's early in the morning. You've taken a phone message for your mother from the garage manager, Mr Marshall. He received your mother's email last week but he didn't have time to reply.

Write a note to your mother. In your note, you should

- say when he phoned
- tell her what he said
- ask her to phone Mr Marshall

Write 35–45 words.

Dear Mum,

23 Best friends?

Grammar

1 Put *which, who, where* or *whose* in the spaces. If it is possible to put nothing, put brackets ( ) around the answer.

I have a great job (**a**) *(which)* I really love. I work as a sports photographer for a big newspaper (**b**) .... has offices all around the world. The office (**c**) .... I work is in the centre of London. I take photos at all the big sports events (**d**) .... take place in the capital and I get quite near to some people (**e**) .... are really famous. The photos (**f**) .... I take are often on the back page of the newspaper. The people (**g**) .... I work with are very friendly, and I have one friend (**h**) .... job is film reviewer, so we sometimes go to the cinema together. The street (**i**) .... my office is has lots of cafés and restaurants (**j**) .... serve really good food, so we often all eat dinner together.

2 Choose a sentence from the box to add to sentences **a–j** as a relative clause. You will need to change some of the words. Add *which* or *who*. If it is possible to put nothing, put brackets ( ) round *which* or *who*.

a The dress *(which) I got for my birthday* no longer fits me.
b The boy .... is now a famous basketball player.
c The parcel .... never arrived.
d Rugby was the sport .... at school.
e The woman .... had curly black hair.
f The film .... was better than I expected.
g The bus .... leaves in ten minutes.
h The man .... made a mistake.
i The book .... has a red cover.
j I'm going to a party ....

> She stole my bag.
> It starts at eight.
> I saw it yesterday.
> ~~I got it for my birthday.~~
> He gave us directions.
> I enjoyed it most.
> It goes to the airport.
> He used to live next door.
> She's lost it.
> We sent it to Sarah.

↘ GF page 212

3 Do this crossword. Some clues have the same answers.

Across

3 This school is really .... from the one I went to before.

8 I can't wait. I'm so excited .... going to Brazil next week.

9, 12 I'm really (12) .... up (9) .... hearing the same jokes all the time.

10 When Fred heard the result of the match, he wasn't very .... about it.

11 My friend has lost the CD I lent her – I'm so angry .... her.

Down

1 There's no space left in this box. It's full .... books.

2 I love this music. I'm really keen .... it.

4 I never know what to say to Carlo. We're not .... in the same things.

5 We're all .... about leaving school.

6 I'm so .... of hearing the planes flying over my flat every day.

7 Thank you .... coming to the party.

8 I'll never beat him. He's so good .... tennis.

Writing

4 Finish these sentences.

a I have a cousin who *wants to be a rock star* .

b I have a friend who ....

c I saw a film which ....

d I once made a journey which ....

e I have a friend whose ....

f I once visited a place where ....

Exam skills

Reading Part 1

Look at the text in each question.
What does it say?
Mark the correct letter A, B or C.

1

> Dear Adrian
> Sorry I wasn't at your party yesterday. I really wanted to come but my uncle arrived and he stayed till late.
> Julien

A Julien didn't go to the party at all.

B Julien's uncle didn't want to go to the party.

C Julien's uncle arrived at the party late.

2

> Sally I got this book for you from the library. I think it's the one you want. If not, I can take it back.
> John

A John wants to read the book after Sally.

B John would like Sally to take the book back for him.

C John is unsure if he has got the right book.

3

> Mum
> I'll be home early on Sunday morning not Saturday evening. You needn't meet me at the airport as I'm getting a lift home.
> Love, Fiona

A Fiona wants her mum to drive to the airport.

B Fiona is arriving later than she expected.

C Fiona needs someone to take her to the airport.

24 I've got an idea

Grammar

1 Put the verb in brackets into the present, past or future passive.

a Gold _wasn't discovered_ (not discover) in California until the eighteenth century.

b I hope my new computer .... (deliver) tomorrow.

c All swimming lessons .... (cancel) today because the teacher is ill.

d In my last job, I .... (pay) much more than I earn here.

e We .... (wake up) by the postman when he rang the doorbell.

f Everyone who joins the club .... (send) a membership card by post.

g The book is so popular I am sure it .... (translate) into other languages in the future.

h I was surprised to see Helen at the party because she .... (not invite).

i Up to 200 kilos of food .... (eat) by an elephant every day.

j Why did you walk here? You .... (offer) a lift by Simon.

2 Justine is a comedian who has recently become very popular. Here is what she wrote in her diary last week.

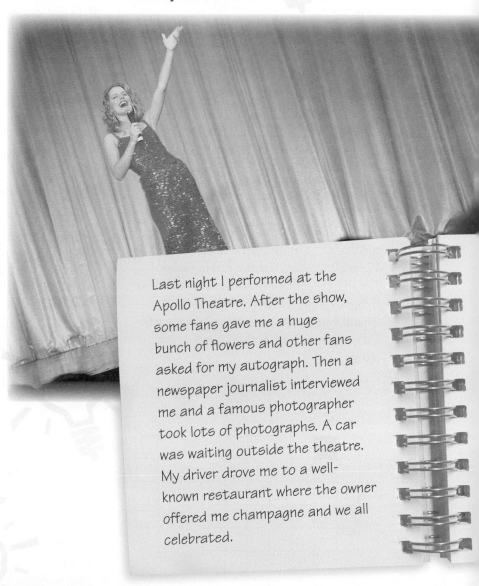

Last night I performed at the Apollo Theatre. After the show, some fans gave me a huge bunch of flowers and other fans asked for my autograph. Then a newspaper journalist interviewed me and a famous photographer took lots of photographs. A car was waiting outside the theatre. My driver drove me to a well-known restaurant where the owner offered me champagne and we all celebrated.

Now fill the spaces in this text so it means the same as the diary above. Use the passive.

Last night I performed at the Apollo Theatre. After the show, **(a)** _I was given a huge bunch of flowers_ by _some fans_ and I **(b)** .... by .... Then I **(c)** .... by .... and lots of photographs **(d)** .... by .... A car was waiting outside the theatre. I **(e)** .... to a well-known restaurant by ...., where I **(f)** .... by .... and we all celebrated.

▶ GF page 213

Vocabulary

3 For each word in list A, find a word in list B which goes with it.

A	B	
ice	oven	ice cream ....
emergency	trolley	....
microwave	officer	....
vacuum	cleaner	....
steam	exit	....
shopping	guitar	....
customs	cream	....
electric	train	....

4 Read this description of an object. Fill in the missing words from the box. What is the object?

can	electric	end	~~long~~	made
put	thin	use		

It's (a) _long_ and (b) ....
One (c) .... is soft.
It's (d) .... of plastic.
It (e) .... be any colour.
Most people (f) .... it in the morning and evening.
You (g) .... it in your mouth and move it around.
Some of them are (h) ....
It's a ....

Pronunciation

5 Which words will you join when you say these sentences? Put a mark between the words and practise saying the sentences.

a I'd like some information about Edinburgh, please.

b I bought an apple pie for my lunch.

c The museum is closed on Thursdays.

d Where is your other sister today?

e My name is Frank and I'm eighteen years old.

Exam skills

Writing Part 1

Here are some sentences about a bicycle.
For each one, complete the second sentence so that it means the same as the first. Use no more than three words.

1 My new bicycle was given to me by my uncle.
My uncle _gave_ .... me my new bicycle.

2 My old bicycle wasn't big enough for me.
My old bicycle was too .... for me.

3 My new bicycle has special wheels.
There .... special wheels on my new bicycle.

4 My new bicycle will be kept in the garage.
I .... my new bicycle in the garage.

5 A friend of mine has a similar bicycle.
One .... has a similar bicycle.

6 My sister said she wanted a new bicycle too.
My sister said, '.................. a new bicycle too.'

25 Shop till you drop

Grammar

1 What did these people say?

a My friend asked me if I had been to the new shoe shop.
She said, '_Have you been_ to the new shoe shop?'

b I asked what time the shop opened in the morning.
I said, '_What time does the shop open_ in the morning?'

c The shop assistant asked me if I wanted to try on some party shoes.
She said, '.. to try on some party shoes?'

d My sister asked where I had bought my new shoes.
She said, '.. new shoes?'

e My mother asked how much I had paid for the shoes.
She said, '.. for the shoes?'

f My friend asked if I would wear my new shoes to her party.
She said, '.. new shoes to my party?'

g My boyfriend asked whether I could dance in such high heels.
He said, '.. in such high heels?'

2 Report these questions.

a He said, 'Are the girls going out?'
He asked _whether the girls were going_ out.

b 'Did you buy anything nice?' asked my friend.
My friend asked me _if I'd bought anything_ nice.

c The manager said to Edward, 'When are you free to start work?'
The manager asked Edward ....
to start work.

d 'Can I speak to your father?' the policeman asked the little girl.
The policeman asked the little girl ....
to her father.

e I said to my brother, 'Why are you looking in my bag?'
I asked my brother .... in my bag.

f 'Have you played basketball before?' the team captain asked me.
The team captain asked me ....
basketball before.

g The receptionist said to the young woman, 'Will you need a taxi after the meeting?'
The receptionist asked the young woman
.... a taxi after the meeting.

3 Rewrite these sentences without *to*.

a Ida gave the money to the assistant.
Ida gave the assistant the money.

b Aphra is sending a text to her father.
....

c Mahmoud was taking a letter to his teacher.
....

d Peter will write a letter to the manager.
....

e Debbie has given the tickets to Tim.
....

f Joe showed the website to his parents.
....

g Beth brought a cup of tea to her mother.
....

4 Complete the sentences with *enough*, *too many* or *too much*.

a I can't come with you tonight. I've got _too much_ work to do.

b I've got .... clothes. I must throw some away.

c I haven't got .... information about the accident, so I can't give an opinion.

d Don't put .... milk in my coffee, please.

e Why are you so tired? Did you have .... homework?

f Have you got .... room for all your things in that case?

g I don't enjoy parties where there are .... people and not .... seats.

↘ GF page 213

Vocabulary

5 Complete the sentences with words from Unit 25, then fit them into the puzzle and find the word down the middle.

1 You help yourself to things in a self-_ _ _ _ _ _ _ shop or café.

2 You can order things by post from a _ _ _ _ _ _ _ _ _ .

3 Don't forget to get a _ _ _ _ _ _ _ when you pay for something.

4 You can use your computer to buy things from a _ _ _ _ _ _ _ .

5 Go to a traditional street _ _ _ _ _ _ if you want to find local goods.

6 You can check whether clothes fit you in the _ _ _ _ _ _ _ _ _ _ _ _ .

7 If you have a problem in a shop, you can ask to speak to the _ _ _ _ _ _ _ .

8 You can find a wide _ _ _ _ _ of clothes in a big store.

9 Some shops keep only a few sizes in _ _ _ _ _ _ .

10 If you want your money back, you should ask for a _ _ _ _ _ _ .

11 When you don't know whether something will fit, ask to _ _ _ _ _ _ _ _ .

Exam skills

Reading Part 1

Look at these signs.
What do they say?
Mark the correct letter A, B or C.

1
All prices include tax and delivery.

A You must pay more if you want things delivered.
B This shop does not charge extra for delivery.
C We add tax to your bill when you pay.

2
Special offers are available every day except Saturday.

A You can buy some things more cheaply on Saturdays.
B There are more bargains on Saturdays.
C Discounts are not offered on Saturdays.

3
ASK A MEMBER OF STAFF FOR HELP IF YOU WISH TO TRY ANY SPORTS EQUIPMENT.

A Don't try the sports equipment on your own.
B Tell the shop assistant if you want to buy some sports equipment.
C Ask the manager to show you our range of sports equipment.

4
We are sorry but we cannot give change for the telephone.

A This telephone takes coins only.
B We do not give refunds for telephones.
C If you want to use the phone, you must have the money you need.

Persuading people

Grammar

1 Put the verbs into the present simple or future.

a If you (phone) me, I (come) and fetch you from college.
If you phone me, I'll come and fetch you from college.

b I (save) money on petrol if I (buy) a smaller car.

c If you (tell) anyone my secret, I (not speak) to you again.

d If the teacher (cancel) the lesson, we (go) to the cinema.

e We (leave) without them if they (not get) here soon.

f If she (move) to that flat, she (have) a long journey to college.

g I (help) you with your science homework if you (teach) me Japanese.

h If he (get) the job, he (earn) lots of money.

2 Put *if* or *when* in each space.

a *If* you lose my MP3 player, I'll never lend you anything again.
b .... I get to the airport, I'll phone you.
c .... I have time, I'll phone Chloe this afternoon.
d .... I'm 17, I'll learn to drive.
e Rob will be pleased .... he wins the race.
f .... the film is over, we'll go and have a pizza.
g Where will you sleep .... the hostel is full?
h I'll hurry .... you wait for me.

3 Rewrite these sentences using *unless*.

a We'll go to the beach tomorrow if it doesn't rain.
We'll go to the beach tomorrow unless it rains.

b You won't get a seat at the concert if you don't buy a ticket in advance.

c If you don't smile at the customers, you won't get a tip.

d She'll have to pay a fine if she doesn't take her library books back today.

e If he doesn't apologise, I won't speak to him again.

f They'll miss the beginning of the film if they don't get here soon.

↘ GF page 213

 Corpus spot

4 Here are some pairs of sentences by PET students. Choose the correct sentence from each pair.

1 a I apologise to tell you I can't go to class tomorrow.
   b I'm sorry to tell you I can't go to class tomorrow.
2 a I recommend that you visit my city.
   b I recommend to you that visit my city.
3 a I want to find out a good cheap desk.
   b I want to find a good cheap desk.
4 a It was raining so I suggested that she could stay there.
   b It was raining so I suggested her to stay there.

Exam skills

Reading Part 4

Read the text and questions below.
For each question, mark the correct letter **A, B, C** or **D.**

A new celebrity magazine called *Their Lives* has just come into our shops. There is, of course, already a wide range of these on the shelves of our newsagents and supermarkets, telling us everything we want to know – and usually things we don't want to know – about people who are famous, and also not so famous.

When I pick up and read a celebrity magazine, I rarely get to the end, as I often don't even know who some of the celebrities are. They have probably been on TV or in a football team for a few weeks but, for me, that doesn't mean everybody wants to know what they eat and where they live. But *Their Lives* kept my attention to the last page. It has about the same number of pages and costs about the same as other celebrity magazines, but it has fewer photographs because it has interviews and reviews as well as the usual kinds of article and pictures. It wasn't until I opened it that I realised that, because it wasn't clear from the cover. Those of you who buy it won't be disappointed, but will it succeed against all those other celebrity magazines out there in the shops? We'll have to wait and see.

1 What is the writer trying to do?
A complain about the design of a new magazine
B suggest how a new magazine could be improved
C persuade people to buy a new magazine
D tell people why a new magazine will succeed

2 What does the writer say about most celebrity magazines?
A They usually show the same people on their pages.
B The celebrities they show aren't very famous.
C They concentrate on famous footballers.
D The information they give is often untrue.

3 What surprised the writer about the new magazine?
A its cover
B its price
C its length
D its contents

Writing Part 1

Here are some sentences about Billy's birthday party. For each question, complete the second sentence so that it means the same as the first. Use no more than three words.

1 Billy asked me if I wanted to come to his party.
Billy said, ' *Do you want* .... to come to my party?'

2 Billy last had a party two years ago.
Billy hasn't had a party .... two years.

3 Billy is two days older than me.
I am two days .... than Billy.

4 Billy was given a present by everyone.
Everyone .... Billy a present.

5 The flat was too small for so many people.
The flat wasn't .... for so many people.

6 If I don't go home soon, I'll be tired tomorrow.
Unless I .... home soon, I'll be tired tomorrow.

Travellers' tales

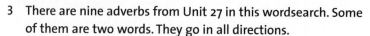

Grammar

1 Complete these sentences with *each*, *every* or *all*. You can use two of the words in some sentences.

a *Each*............ of the teams of archaeologists comes from a different country.

b .... these buildings have been buried for hundreds of years.

c .... archaeologist hopes to find a rare and beautiful object.

d We photograph .... the things we find very carefully.

e We mark .... of the objects on a map to show where we found it.

f There is a small label on .... object.

g .... the work will be described in a book.

2 Complete these sentences using a verb from the box + *myself*, *yourself*, etc. Two sentences also need *not*.

ask	enjoy	help	hurt
look after	~~talk about~~		talk to

a My professor is a good teacher and she encourages us to *talk about ourselves*.... and our work.

b She really .... when she visited the Roman palace we had found.

c She fell into a hole but luckily she .... badly.

d The archaeologists have to .... and cook their own meals.

e Sometimes the professor .... to my sandwiches when she's hungry.

f One of my colleagues often .... when he's working.

g Why .... what people think about him?

↘ GF page 213

Vocabulary

3 There are nine adverbs from Unit 27 in this wordsearch. Some of them are two words. They go in all directions.

A	S	B	C	D	Q	V	E	R	N	L	U	I	O	P
L	U	C	K	I	L	Y	Y	L	L	A	U	T	C	A
S	R	D	F	N	G	I	P	X	A	W	N	E	D	C
K	P	J	H	F	G	F	D	S	A	S	F	P	O	I
C	R	B	N	A	M	I	N	V	F	R	O	T	U	H
F	I	G	H	C	U	K	M	N	B	B	R	D	L	Y
E	S	A	I	T	L	H	J	N	V	U	T	R	S	E
R	I	B	O	X	Y	Y	L	I	K	C	U	L	N	U
U	N	V	G	U	L	S	O	F	I	B	N	O	J	M
S	G	O	F	C	O	U	R	S	E	A	A	D	D	S
A	L	L	I	M	S	A	M	E	N	T	T	C	U	O
W	Y	P	L	L	E	N	Y	R	O	F	E	A	P	M
H	E	L	Y	I	M	U	E	S	K	U	L	T	T	A
U	F	O	R	T	U	N	A	T	E	L	Y	G	Y	N

Pronunciation

4 Read the sentences below and mark the sounds /eə/ as in *fair* or /ɪə/ as in *dear* in different ways. Then copy the words into the correct columns.

a <u>Ear</u>rings like these are <u>rare</u>.

b These are the chairs where we were sitting.

c There were tears in her eyes when she spoke.

d Our friends are going to share their food with us.

e I don't care if I tear my jeans, they're very old.

f We're all feeling cheerful.

g I fear there may be bears near here.

/eə/ fair	/ɪə/ dear
rare	*earrings*

Exam skills

Look at the sentences below about a town called Stevening.
Read the text to decide if each sentence is correct or incorrect.
If it is correct, write A.
If it is incorrect, write B.

1 There is a good variety of places to stay in Stevening. *A*
2 The Tourist Information Office charges for booking rooms.
3 You can rent a tent at the campsite.
4 There used to be a traditional market where Stevening Mall is now.
5 You can park in St Hugh's Square before 9 am.
6 You can buy medicine in the Mall.
7 If you join the Sports Club, it is cheaper during the evening than during the day.
8 You can register for swimming lessons at the Leisure Centre.
9 You must buy a ticket for the Kerrow Hills bus at the Tourist Information Office.
10 The train stops near the top of Kerrow Mountain.

WELCOME TO STEVENING

The town offers excellent accommodation at all prices. You can stay in a simple but comfortable family home or small guesthouse, or try the international dining room and beautiful rooms at the Grand Hotel. You can book a room by phoning or emailing the owner. You can get a list from the Tourist Information Office in St Hugh's Square, which is open between 9 and 5 on weekdays. For a small fee, the staff can make reservations while you wait.

There is also a campsite near the town. Space is usually available for small tents, but large groups should contact the manager in advance to check that there will be room for them.

Stevening has two main shopping areas, the new Stevening Mall and the traditional market area, which includes St Hugh's Square and several attractive narrow streets around it. Please note that motor vehicles are only allowed into St Hugh's Square between 7 pm and 9 am. The Mall has over forty shops, including a department store, clothes shops for all ages, sports shops, a chemist and a supermarket.

For sport, visit the Stevening Leisure Centre, which offers indoor tennis, volleyball and a fitness centre. You can pay for a half day, or join the Sports Club, which allows you to use the facilities all day for no charge and at a special discount in the evenings.

The swimming pool is open from May to September. Classes are held in the pool between 3 and 5 every afternoon except Sundays. Details of courses are available at the Leisure Centre but it is only possible to book a course at the pool office.

From Stevening, it is easy to visit a number of places of interest. The peace of the Kerrow Hills is a short free bus ride from the town centre. Maps can be obtained from the Tourist Information Office. Keen walkers may climb up Kerrow Mountain, but less active visitors can also enjoy the wonderful views by taking the little train which stops just below the top of the mountain and walking the last few metres.

28

What would you do?

Grammar

1 Put the verbs in brackets into the correct form. Use the second conditional.

a I (go) to the theatre every week if I (live) in the city.
   I'd go to the theatre every week if I lived in the city.

b If I (not be) so untidy, I (not lose) things all the time.
   ....
   ....

c I (invite) my neighbour to my party if she (be) more friendly.
   ....
   ....

d If Roseanne (find) a job, she (have) more pocket money.
   ....
   ....

e If I (have) a copy of the book you want, I (lend) it to you.
   ....
   ....

f If Amy (not use) a computer, her work (be) very difficult to read.
   ....
   ....

g I (give) you all a lift if I (own) a bigger car.
   ....
   ....

h If I (know) the answer, I (tell) you.
   ....
   ....

2 Finish each sentence below by choosing an ending from the box. Put the verb in brackets into the correct form.

> (have) a good voice.   (be) on Saturday.
> (use) a diary.   (want) to ask any questions.
> (cross) the border.   (practise) hard.
> (trust) him.   (feel) warm.

a I'd join a band if I *had a good voice.* ....

b More people would come if the party
   ....

c You will need your passport if you
   ....

d I'll email you tomorrow if I
   ....

e We'll go swimming with you if the water
   ....

f I would lend Peter the money if I
   ....

g Juan wouldn't forget everything if he
   ....

h The school team will win the next match if they ....

3 Look at the letters which are underlined. Write the words in full.

a We've decided not to come with you.
   have

b My friend's moving to another town.
   ....

c If I had a mobile phone with me, I'd send them a text message.
   ....

d She's never visited us before.
   ....

e They'd finished eating when we arrived.
   ....

f Charlotte's got a new camera.
   ....

g If you give me your address, I'll send you a postcard.
   ....

h Stephanie's lent me her jacket.
   ....

i We realised we'd forgotten to bring the tickets when we got to the cinema.
   ....

j I think we're nearly there – I recognise that building.
   ....

⬎ GF page 214

Vocabulary

4 Complete the text with *at*, *by*, *in* or *on*.

When I was nineteen I saw an advert for a job as a nanny in France. I phoned (**a**) ...*at*... once. The family said they had someone (**b**) .... present but I could start in July. They sent me some photos of their house and the children. I decided to travel there (**c**) .... sea and I bought my ticket (**d**) .... advance because it was cheaper. The mother and father were (**e**) .... work most of the day and I stayed (**f**) .... home with twin babies and a little girl. They expected me to babysit (**g**) .... least two evenings a week and they both travelled abroad quite often (**h**) .... business. The little girl was (**i**) .... school in the mornings. I knew the town very well (**j**) .... the end because I went everywhere (**k**) .... bus or (**l**) .... foot. I had a really good time although it was hard work and now I go to France (**m**) .... holiday whenever I can.

5 Write the missing words. They all have the letter *i* in them. Use the diagram to help you.

1 Would you like to ...*experience*... the life of the rich and famous?
2 If you're famous, you mustn't make a .... when you choose what to wear.
3 How would you feel if you were .... for choosing a film star's clothes?
4 Famous people can't afford to look bad in ....
5 What .... do you need to become a bodyguard?
6 You might be able to visit some wonderful places when your boss takes a ....
7 Some jobs allow you to enjoy travelling like a .... without being famous yourself.
8 Would you be ready for work in the morning if you'd spent the evening at a .... ?

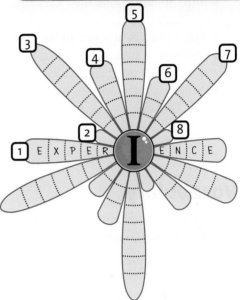

Exam skills

Writing Part 3

This is part of an email you receive from an English friend.

> I want to get a weekend job so I have my own money to go out and buy things. My parents think I won't have enough time to do my school work. Do you have a job? What do you think I should do?

Complete the reply using the expressions below and your own ideas. Write about 100 words.

I don't have a job but I would like to work in a … I would spend the money on … OR I work every … in a … and I earn … I spend it on …
I think it is important to … because …
If you get a job, you will …
If you don't get a job, you will …
So I think you should/shouldn't …

> Dear Sam
> It was good to hear from you. ....
> ....
> ....
> ....
> ....

29 What's on the menu?

Grammar

1 Rewrite these questions using the beginnings given.

a What is this cheese called? Can you remember *what this cheese is called?*

b Where are the beans? Do you know

c How much does steak cost? Can you tell me

d How should I cook this? Can you explain

e Have you got any vegetarian dishes? I'd like to know

f When will strawberries be available? Can you find out

2 Read these statements and write short answers agreeing with them. Use *So do I* etc. or *Nor do I* etc. + the words given.

a I drink coffee when I'm revising. (I)
So do I.

b Polly didn't enjoy her meal. (Mina)
Nor did Mina.

c We don't eat meat every day. (we)

d I haven't had breakfast. (I)

e I'm going to have a slice of cake. (we)

f Hattie will make some food for the party. (Jane)

g I can't understand this recipe. (I)

h The waiter was very rude. (manager)

i Anthony hasn't learnt to cook yet. (Guy)

↘ GF page 214

Vocabulary

3 Solve these clues and write the missing words in the squares. Each word begins with the last letter of the word before it. The last word ends with the first letter in the puzzle.

1 Some people put c_r_e_a_m in their coffee.
2 I enjoy going out for a _ _ _ _ in a restaurant.
3 There's a _ _ _ _ of bread on the table.
4 Europeans usually use knives and _ _ _ _ _ to eat with.
5 We can make a _ _ _ _ _ with lettuce and other vegetables.
6 Some people go on a special _ _ _ _ to improve their health.
7 _ _ _ _ _ _ _ _ are red, but are they fruit or vegetables?
8 Some people like food with hot _ _ _ _ _ _ in it.
9 Sugar is _ _ _ _ _ _ .
10 This food _ _ _ _ _ _ delicious. What is it?
11 We often have _ _ _ _ for our first course at dinner.
12 It's a lovely day. Let's go for a _ _ _ _ _ _ in the country.

C											
R				
E				
A				
M				

Exam skills

Reading Part 2

The people below all want to go out for a meal.
Read the eight descriptions of restaurants (A–H).
Decide which restaurant would be the most suitable
for each person or group (1–5).

1 Stan and Hilda want to celebrate their wedding anniversary by having dinner with their children and grandchildren that evening. They'd like to find a restaurant which offers lots of different kinds of food and isn't too expensive.

2 Richard is travelling alone and needs somewhere to eat dinner. He is looking for a quiet restaurant where he can try typical local food. He isn't worried how much it costs.

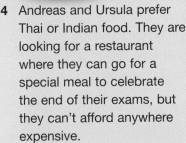

3 Simone and Margarita want to find somewhere which serves light snacks during the day. They don't want to spend a long time there.

4 Andreas and Ursula prefer Thai or Indian food. They are looking for a restaurant where they can go for a special meal to celebrate the end of their exams, but they can't afford anywhere expensive.

5 The Hamed family need a restaurant where they can have a good breakfast before catching a train at 8 am. Some members of the family are vegetarians.

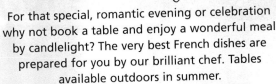

A *Toni and Tim, High Street*
For that special, romantic evening or celebration why not book a table and enjoy a wonderful meal by candlelight? The very best French dishes are prepared for you by our brilliant chef. Tables available outdoors in summer.

B THE SINGING BIRD, Station Road
Our experienced chefs prepare real Thai food at unbelievably low prices. You will always remember a meal you have eaten here and will want to come back again and again. Open noon to midnight.

C *The Old Garden, Orchard Avenue*
All our dishes are traditional ones from this part of the country and the food is freshly prepared for each customer. Enjoy a peaceful meal in beautiful surroundings. We're not the cheapest, but we're probably the best! Open 7 pm – 11 pm

D **Henry's Snackbar, College Road**
Choose from delicious burgers, hot dogs, curries and sandwiches. All prepared with the best local bread, meat and vegetables and cooked in our own kitchen for you to take home and enjoy. Phone orders welcome. Open 11 am till midnight.

E **Juno's Foods, High Street**
We serve salads, soup and delicious sandwiches from 9 till 9. Plenty of choice at any time. Vegetarians welcome. Our young staff offer fast, friendly service in a clean, modern restaurant.

F **The Apple Tree,** College Road
For a takeaway meal to remember. The best of Indian or Thai food, carefully prepared for you to enjoy in your own home. Ask about our special midweek prices and student discounts.

G The Hot Pot, Market Street
Full range of hot food always available, including children's menu and vegetarian. Open 6 am till 5 pm every day. Children's playground and video games. Takeaway also available.

H *The Golden Rose, Station Road*
Open midday to midnight. A lively and amusing place for a meal. Traditional local food, special foreign dishes and vegetarian. Special discounts for groups and parties. Live music. Children welcome.

Blue for a boy, pink for a girl?

Grammar

1 Rewrite the underlined parts of these sentences using *hardly*.

a I've only been to Naples once, so I <u>don't know it well</u>. I've only been to Naples once, so I
hardly know it.

b The road was very quiet, so I <u>didn't see many cars</u>.
....

c He was so shy he <u>only spoke a few words</u>.
....

d We were so busy revising we <u>only went out once</u>.
....

e I was bored at school because we <u>learnt little that was new</u>.
....

f The song was in Spanish, so I <u>only understood a bit of it</u>.
....

↘ **GF page 214**

2 Rewrite these sentences beginning with *Before* or *After*.

Exam skills

a enter the exam room / check that you have everything you need
Before *entering the exam room, check that you have everything you need.*

b leave home / eat a light meal
Before ....
....

c start to write / look through the whole paper quickly
Before ....
....

d answer a question / read the text
Before ....
....

e complete each part of the exam / check how much time remains
After ....
....

f write all your answers / read them carefully
After ....
....

g hand in your paper / forget about it and relax!
After ....
....

3 Complete the sentences with the verb in brackets in the correct form.

a I'll call you when I *reach* .... (reach) the hostel.

b She .... (move) from here a year ago.

c While I was walking home I .... (lose) my front door key.

d When I arrived at the cinema, the film .... (already start).

e He won't leave until his friends .... (phone).

f I .... (own) this scooter for two years.

g We'll miss the bus if we .... (not hurry).

↘ **Corpus spot**

4 Here are some sentences by PET students. Correct the mistakes.

a I make my homework in my bedroom.

b I'm living in a hotel in the moment.

c A tourist guide said us that the building was very old.

d We arrived to a big lake and had a picnic.

e She is very well at horse-riding.

f I slept very bad in the old bed.

g I think we will pass a good time on our holiday.

h There is a TV so I won't feel boring at night.

i The sun was shinning in the morning.

j I advice you to choose a big city to visit.

k I decided to left my friends in the café and go home.

l He asked me to going out with him.

m I used to cycling every day in my country.

n In winter you can make snowboarding or skiing.

o I hope you to enjoy the party.

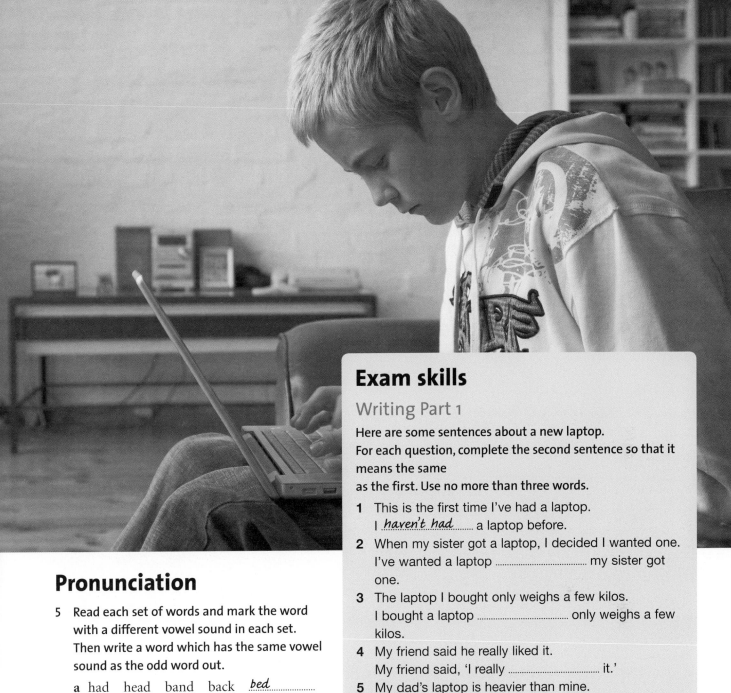

Pronunciation

5 Read each set of words and mark the word
   with a different vowel sound in each set.
   Then write a word which has the same vowel
   sound as the odd word out.

   a had   head   band   back   *bed*.................

   b much   some   put   done   ....

   c heart   heard   can't   half   ....

   d walk   short   caught   down   ....

   e hair   wear   their   we're   ....

   f talk   bird   nurse   word   ....

   g right   sign   buy   key   ....

   h plane   way   have   brain   ....

Exam skills

Writing Part 1

Here are some sentences about a new laptop.
For each question, complete the second sentence so that it
means the same
as the first. Use no more than three words.

1 This is the first time I've had a laptop.
   I *haven't had*............ a laptop before.

2 When my sister got a laptop, I decided I wanted one.
   I've wanted a laptop .... my sister got
   one.

3 The laptop I bought only weighs a few kilos.
   I bought a laptop .... only weighs a few
   kilos.

4 My friend said he really liked it.
   My friend said, 'I really .... it.'

5 My dad's laptop is heavier than mine.
   My laptop isn't as .... my dad's.

6 I'm allowed to take my laptop to school if I don't
   cycle there.
   I'm allowed to take my laptop to school
   .... I cycle there.

Writing Part 2

You went to a restaurant with your family on Saturday.

Write an email to your friend Sara. In your email, you should

• tell her why you liked the restaurant

• invite her to go there with you

• explain where the restaurant is

Write 35–45 words.

Answer key

Unit 1

Vocabulary

1 b cycling   **c** horse riding   **d** skiing
  e tennis   **f** volleyball   **g** windsurfing

2 b racket   **c** board   **d** brushes; stones
  e wear; summer

3 b cycling   **c** dangerous   **d** steep
  e winter   **f** ice   **g** fall   **h** wear   **i** cover

Grammar

4 b There are usually lots of people …
  c My sister is always happy …
  d Do your parents sometimes play …
  e We usually go horse riding …
  f Our dog doesn't usually like …, but he always enjoys …
  g My brother never watches sport …

5 2 a/d/e   **3** d/e   **4** b   **5** e/d   **6** c

Writing

6 Any suitable answer using present simple.

Exam skills

1 C   **2** A

Unit 2

Grammar

1 b ~~Does~~ **Would** Amy like to go to the disco with us?
  I think she wants ~~staying~~ **to stay** at home.
  c My brother would like ~~going~~ **to go** to the disco with you but ~~he~~ he's got homework.
  d How many children ~~have~~ **has** your sister **got**?
  e ~~Do~~ **Does** Paul ~~likes~~ **like** pop music?
  f What ~~would~~ **do** you like doing on holiday?

Pronunciation

2 a F<u>ew</u> st<u>u</u>dents c<u>o</u>me to this cl<u>u</u>b <u>o</u>n M<u>o</u>ndays.
  b They listen to p<u>o</u>p m<u>u</u>sic and disc<u>u</u>ss the f<u>u</u>ture.
  c D<u>oe</u>s it c<u>o</u>st m<u>u</u>ch to bel<u>o</u>ng to the cl<u>u</u>b?

/ʌ/ sun	/juː/ new	/ɒ/ hot
come	few	on
club	students	pop
Mondays	music	cost
discuss	future	belong
does		
much		

Vocabulary

3 b friendly   **c** busy   **d** tidy   **e** serious
  f hard-working   **g** shy   **h** happy

4 b plans   **c** I've   **d** like   **e** playing
  f watching   **g** I'd   **h** cycling   **i** name
  j Would

6 I'm enjoying my holiday in Ireland.
  We swim in the morning and then have lunch at a restaurant called Patrick's Garden.
  My parents like visiting museums(,) but I don't.
  I sometimes drive my parents' car to Dublin and meet my cousins there.
  We're flying to America next week.
  Ryan

Unit 3

Grammar

1 b is/'s happening   **c** is/'s not / isn't moving
  d is/'s driving   **e** am/'m walking
  f are/'re holding   **g** are trying

2 b are watching   **c** is/'s looking
  d isn't / 's not landing   **e** is/'s keeping
  f is/'s opening   **g** is/'s hanging
  h is/'s taking   **i** is/'s going   **j** are waving
  k are smiling

3 *Possible answers*
  b usually drives a taxi. / is/'s playing chess.
  c usually plays football. / is/'s opening a restaurant.
  d usually studies in a laboratory.
    This week he's visiting his family.
  e usually writes computer games.
    This week she's studying Chinese.
  f usually interviews famous people.
    This week he's reading books and cooking for his family.

4 b I always count   **c** I open
  d Are you counting   **e** Mum's counting
  f your mother always goes   **g** Tony's going
  h Tony always puts   **i** washes   **j** I'm putting
  k I'm carrying   **l** We always open
  m You aren't opening   **n** I'm putting
  o I'm walking   **p** I'm opening
  q some people are coming   **r** you're not helping

5 c they don't   **d** he is   **e** she doesn't
  f they are   **g** I do   **h** they aren't   **i** she does

Writing
6 Any suitable answers using present simple and present continuous.

Vocabulary
7 b shop assistant   **c** journalist   **d** hairdresser
  e photographer   **f** engineer   **g** sales person

Unit 4
Vocabulary
1 b September; February   **c** summer
  d August   **e** Saturdays   **f** tomorrow
  g January   **h** Tuesday; Thursday   **i** April

2

P	B	O	S	M	U	S	M	A	G	I	C
H	L	L	P	U	C	R	I	M	E	I	I
I	T	A	D	S	O	W	R	D	A	P	N
N	Q	J	Y	I	M	O	Z	A	T	E	M
T	C	O	N	C	E	R	T	M	R	R	M
E	I	Y	S	A	D	A	M	Y	O	F	A
R	R	G	H	L	Y	A	R	E	C	O	R
V	C	U	A	L	H	P	N	U	K	R	E
A	U	F	B	A	N	D	K	C	C	M	E
L	S	D	E	U	S	R	O	U	E	R	A

interval, play, dance, comedy, circus, cinema, concert, musical, perform, magic, rock, band

Grammar
3 On Tuesday we are visiting museums in London.
On Tuesday evening we are seeing a play at the theatre in London.
On Wednesday you are spending the day at school.
On Wednesday evening we are going to the cinema.
On Thursday you are doing different sports in the activity centre.
On Thursday evening you are having a meal in a restaurant with my family.
On Friday morning you are going shopping.
On Friday afternoon we are preparing for a party.
On Friday evening we are having a party.
On Saturday morning you are leaving for an early flight.

4 b in June   **c** at six o'clock   **d** correct
  e at the weekend   **f** at Christmas
  g at the weekend   **h** in this afternoon
  i correct   **j** on 25th March

5 c At   **d** on   **e** on   **f** –   **g** at   **h** on
  i in   **j** in   **k** on   **l** in

Exam skills
Sample answer
Dear David
I can't see you next Saturday because I'm visiting my uncle with my family. It's his birthday. Can you meet me on Sunday morning? I'd like to go to the swimming pool or play tennis.
Best wishes
Fabrizio

Unit 5
Grammar
1

a	some
country	advice
holiday	bread
journey	chocolate
motorway	furniture
shoe	information
toothbrush	luggage
tram	money
wheel	music

2 b any   **c** some   **d** a   **e** any   **f** some
  g some   **h** any   **i** any   **j** some
  k a   **l** any   **m** some

3 b a lot of   **c** much   **d** a little   **e** much
  f many   **g** a few   **h** many

4 *Suggested answers*
  b (to wear) a helmet.
  c to open the window.
  d to wash them.
  e pay / bring any money.
  f to mend/fix it.
  g (to buy) some flour.
  h a key.

5 b needs   **c** Do you need
  d needn't / don't need to   **e** needs
  f needn't / don't need to   **g** Does he need

Vocabulary
6 b coach   **c** taxi   **d** helicopter
  e motorbike   **f** ferry   **g** bicycle
  h scooter   **i** train   **j** lorry

Unit 6
Grammar
1 b tidied; arrived   **c** Did (your brother) enjoy
  d didn't jump   **e** didn't arrest
  f Did (you) invite

2 b began **c** made **d** was **e** Were
f Did (you) feel **g** didn't find
h Did (you) spend **i** told **j** Was
k lost; weren't

3 b had **c** were **d** didn't go **e** enjoyed
f wrote **g** learnt/learned **h** worked
i was **j** introduced **k** divorced **l** met
m became **n** wrote **o** died

4 b tired **c** interested **d** amusing **e** bored
f boring **g** amused

5

A	B	E	C	A	M	E	E	M	A	D	E
T	B	E	W	B	W	A	R	E	D	E	D
C	F	P	G	O	T	E	A	T	O	O	K
E	L	Q	X	A	Y	P	L	A	M	P	N
F	W	S	A	D	N	P	S	B	I	L	E
D	E	T	C	M	Z	O	T	E	D	I	W
H	R	L	E	D	T	E	U	D	F	I	N
I	E	U	T	F	S	D	D	S	S	T	Y
J	M	N	M	O	O	F	I	H	X	U	E
X	E	A	J	U	L	A	E	O	V	A	W
W	N	R	K	N	R	D	D	B	I	L	T
Z	O	V	V	D	S	I	T	S	K	E	D

became, (came), made, met, began, took, knew, got, felt, were, went, found, told, studied, (died), wished, lost, ran

Vocabulary

6 b boring **c** laptop **d** teenager **e** traffic
f laboratory

Pronunciation

7

/d/ arrived	/t/ helped	/ɪd/ started
enjoyed	kicked	ended
happened	jumped	included
imagined	liked	needed
opened	walked	visited
travelled	watched	wanted

Unit 7

Grammar

1 b The city is busier than the countryside.
c China is bigger than Britain.
d Newspapers are not as/so expensive as magazines.
e Hockey is not as/so popular as football.
f My father is older than / not as old as my teacher.
g Horses are not as/so dangerous as elephants.
h A train is faster than a bicycle.
i I am taller than / not as tall as my best friend.

2 b over **c** up **d** down **e** across
f off **g** through

3 b The school is next to the skateboard park.
c The car park is opposite the railway station.
d The park is behind the supermarket.
e The library is between the petrol station and the shopping centre.

Vocabulary

4 ↓ Start

H	↓N	W	O	T	E	K	←R
A	I	↓E	E	R	G	←N	A
L	G	N	↓O	I	←K	I	M
L	H	G	S	■	N	M	U
I	T	R	K	■	A	M	E
G	C	O	→C	E	↑R	I	S
H	L	→U	B	U	S	↑W	U
T	→S	T	A	D	I	U	↑M

Writing

5 *Suggested answers*
a Come out of the shopping centre into Bank Street. Turn right at the roundabout. Go past the theatre. The railway station is on the right.
b Come out of the supermarket and turn right. Go down the road to the crossroads. Turn left. The library is on your left next to the petrol station.
c Come out of the railway station and turn left. Go straight down the road. Go straight ahead at the roundabout. Take the second turning on the right. The skateboard park is on the left next to the school.

Pronunciation

6

/ɔː/ more	/aʊ/ town
walk	*how*
tall	house
board	now
bought	found
sport	down

Unit 8

Grammar

1 **b** has/'s made   **c** Have (you) enjoyed
   d hasn't written   **e** have gone
   f haven't bought   **g** has begun
   h have stopped   **i** have/'ve found
   j Has (José) sent

2 **c** She's already decided where to have the party.
   d She hasn't hired a disco yet.
   e She's already planned the food.
   f She's already ordered the drinks.
   g She hasn't chosen a new dress yet.

3 **b** I've just taken   **c** She's just had
   d they've just booked   **e** I've just passed
   f he's just bought

Vocabulary

4 Happy anniversary   Have a good journey
   Enjoy your meal   Well done
   Good luck   Have a nice weekend

5 **b** explain   **c** invite   **d** describe   **e** thank
   f suggest   **g** apologise

Exam skills

Sample answer
I'm very sorry I can't come to the barbecue because my landlady is taking me to the seaside that day. There's a disco at my college on Fridays. The other students say it's good. We can go together. What do you think?
Best wishes
Turan

Unit 9

Grammar

1 *Suggested answers*
You'd better take the car to the garage.
You'd better buy some more petrol.
You should buy a new lamp.
Why don't you play basketball in the garden next time?
You'd better apologise to the neighbours for the noise.
You should buy some more food.
You shouldn't tell Mum and Dad about the party.
You shouldn't stay in the house alone again.
You shouldn't have another party.

2 **b** I/we didn't   **c** it has   **d** I haven't   **e** she does
   f we/you don't   **g** they were   **h** I did
   i he hasn't   **j** she hasn't

Pronunciation

3

/e/ help	/eɪ/ play
bread	*always*
breakfast	break
fell	came
friend	sale
help	say
said	train

Vocabulary

4 **b** a temperature   **c** sick   **d** toothache
   e hurt / are sore   **f** a headache   **g** hurt
   h sore finger   **i** a cough

5

Exam skills

1 A 2 B 3 D

Unit 10

Grammar

1 **b** correct
   c I ~~didn't eat~~ anything since midday. *haven't eaten*
   d ~~They've started~~ their course in September. *They started*
   e correct
   f The other students ~~have left~~ half an hour ago. *left*
   g ~~Did you live~~ here all your life? *Have you lived*
   h The school ~~has opened~~ in 1990. *opened*

2 **b** ever **c** for **d** since **e** ago **f** yet

3 **b** gone **c** been **d** been **e** gone
   f gone **g** been

4 **a** She **bought** a lot of presents.
   b The policeman **caught** the thief.
   c You have **chosen** a good school.
   d We **drank** coffee and talked.
   e My father **gave** me this watch.
   f I haven't **written** an answer to your letter.

Pronunciation

5 **b** The tram pass<u>es</u> our school, but the bus<u>es</u> don't.
   c She catch<u>es</u> the early train on Monday<u>s</u>.
   d My brother'<u>s</u> friend keep(s) snake(s) in the bedroom.
   e The weather change<u>s</u> quickly in the mountain<u>s</u>.
   f When my sister sing<u>s</u>, the dog go<u>es</u> out of the room.

/s/ books	/z/ schools	/ɪz/ glasses
cups	*mugs*	*dishes*
keeps	Mondays	passes
snakes	brother's	buses
	mountains	catches
	sings	changes
	goes	

Vocabulary

6 **b** friend **c** application **d** signature
   e Unfortunately **f** hostel **g** attend
   h accommodation **i** arrival **j** sincerely

7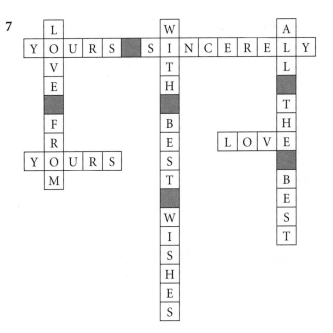

Unit 11

Grammar

1 **b** is cleaned **c** are printed **d** are invited
   e are made **f** is chosen **g** are practised
   h are stopped

2 **b** Sergio is the heaviest.
   c Adam is the oldest.
   d The Caspian Sea is the largest.
   e Buenos Aires is the farthest/furthest (from Rome).
   f Maurice Greene is the best (runner).
   g A glass of juice is the most expensive (drink).
   h San Francisco is the hottest (place) in August.

Vocabulary

3

A	X	T	D	E	J	C	E	F	A	Y	R
N	R	U	S	M	N	I	L	D	W	T	H
A	G	S	E	B	B	G	I	S	Q	D	S
I	P	Q	I	R	R	U	L	M	B	F	I
S	O	U	T	H	A	F	R	I	C	A	N
S	L	V	A	W	Z	W	S	I	S	S	A
U	I	L	L	Y	I	Z	P	O	V	H	P
R	S	L	I	Q	L	V	E	N	J	W	S
J	H	I	A	P	I	K	H	H	K	J	O
M	A	P	N	E	A	R	U	T	O	B	C
E	N	X	Y	A	N	A	I	D	N	I	X

William Shakespeare – English
Pablo Picasso – Spanish
Frédéric Chopin – Polish
Nelson Mandela – South African
Leonardo da Vinci – Italian
Mahatma Gandhi – Indian
Leo Tolstoy – Russian
Pelé – Brazilian

Pronunciation
4 b ch **c** sh **d** sh sh **e** ch **f** ch
g ch **h** ch **i** sh

/tʃ/ cheese	/ʃ/ shoe
change	*ship*
cheapest	wash
much	shower
chips	shoulders
watch	sugar
cheerful	station
coach	
chicken	

Writing
5 b 3,589 **c** 35,805 **d** 350,859
e 385 **f** 38,509 **g** 3,980

Exam skills
2 not as big/large **3** smallest (boy)
4 as tiring as **5** gives **6** drives

Unit 12
Grammar
1 b Billy was riding his motorbike.
c Carla was getting dressed.
d Danny was eating breakfast.
e Erica was looking for her mobile.
f Freddie was phoning his girlfriend.
g Glenda was playing her guitar.
h Hugo was listening to Glenda.

2 b While Sandy was sitting in the classroom, Moira was dreaming about Scotland.
c While Sandy was doing her homework, Moira was making breakfast for her cousins.
d While Sandy was sitting in the cinema, Moira was walking on the beach.
e While Sandy was getting ready for bed, Moira was sailing round the Bay of Islands.
f While Sandy was sleeping, Moira was watching a rugby match.

Pronunciation
3 b I can't p<u>u</u>ll these b<u>oo</u>ts off.
c He t<u>oo</u>k my bl<u>ue</u> sh<u>oe</u>s.
d P<u>u</u>t the b<u>oo</u>ks in the b<u>oo</u>t of the car.
e The r<u>oo</u>m was f<u>u</u>ll so I st<u>oo</u>d on a st<u>oo</u>l.

/uː/ two		/ʊ/ look	
school	shoes	*good*	books
food	boot	pull	full
boots	room	took	stood
blue	stool	put	

Writing
4 *Sample answer*
The television programme was called *Mystery in Mexico* and lots of famous actors were in it. It was fiction and it was part of a series. It was an adventure story about a missing diamond and it took place in Mexico City. The hero was Antonio, a Mexican detective. It was an exciting story and I enjoyed it very much.

Vocabulary
5

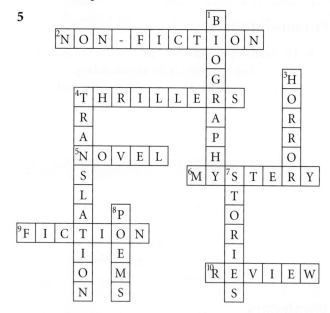

Exam skills
The correct order is:
2 d **3** c **4** h **5** a **6** e **7** k
8 f **9** i **10** g **11** b

A strange event

When I was six my parents took my little sister, Agnes, and me to the seaside one afternoon. My father was looking round the town while my mother was watching Agnes and me on the beach. After a few minutes, my mother realised that Agnes wasn't with us. We looked around and we saw her. She was walking towards a busy road. It was very dangerous. Suddenly she stopped and walked back to us. 'Where's Daddy?' she asked.

When my father arrived a few minutes later, Agnes asked him, 'Did you call me?'

'No,' said my father and Agnes looked surprised. 'Well, who did? Because that's why I didn't cross the road,' she said.

Unit 13

Grammar

1 c on top of   **d** above   **e** opposite
    f side by side   **g** below   **h** over   **i** between

2 b can't   **c** must   **d** can't   **e** could

Pronunciation

3 b There's usually some juice in the fridge.
   c Can you join us to look round the college?
   d The weather is generally good in August, but not in January.
   e We must measure the lounge before we make a decision about furniture.
   f What age was John when he made that journey?

/ʒ/ television	/dʒ/ joke
revision	*pages*
usually	juice
measure	fridge
decision	join
	college
	generally
	January
	lounge
	age
	John
	journey

Vocabulary

4 *Suggested answers*
   living room: sofa, (arm)chair, table, television, bookshelves, mirror, rug, carpet
   bathroom: shower, bath, toilet, basin, mirror

   kitchen: cooker, fridge, cupboards, sink, dishwasher, washing machine
   bedroom: bed, bedside table, wardrobe/cupboards, pillows, mirror, curtains

5

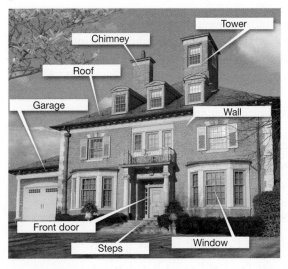

Exam skills

2 A   **3** B   **4** C   **5** D   **6** A   **7** B   **8** C
9 A   **10** D

Unit 14

Grammar

1 *Suggested answers*
Daniela used to travel to school in an expensive car.
Daniela used to wear designer clothes.
Daniela used to go to a luxury hotel for her holiday.
Daniela used to have lots of pocket money.
Daniela didn't use to help in a shop.
Daniela didn't use to walk to school.
Daniela didn't use to wear her sister's old clothes.
Daniela didn't use to go camping for her holiday.
Daniela didn't use to share a bedroom with her sister.
Alma used to help in a shop.
Alma used to walk to school.
Alma used to wear her sister's old clothes.
Alma used to go camping for her holiday.
Alma used to share a bedroom with her sister.
Alma didn't use to travel to school in an expensive car.
Alma didn't use to wear designer clothes.
Alma didn't use to go to a luxury hotel for her holiday.
Alma didn't use to have lots of pocket money.

2 *Suggested answers*
   c far   **d** old enough   **e** late/slow
   f dark enough   **g** loud enough   **h** expensive
   i small/short   **j** cold enough

3 **b** loud rock music   **c** lovely long silver earrings
    d expensive plastic toys   **e** new blue cotton dress
    f short black hair

Vocabulary

4 *Suggested answers*
   The woman is wearing black trousers with a white
   belt, a white T-shirt/top and she is wearing some
   beads round her neck. She is also wearing a white hat
   and sunglasses and black shoes/boots with high heels.
   The man is wearing a striped shirt and a tie, jeans
   with a black belt and a jacket. He is wearing white
   trainers.

5

T	P	M	K	L	E	O	Y	M
P	B	U	M	G	W	R	E	D
N	W	O	R	B	O	A	U	H
U	S	E	J	P	L	N	L	B
B	Y	W	Y	O	L	G	B	J
T	W	H	I	T	E	E	K	P
P	A	L	R	I	Y	O	F	I
L	N	E	E	R	G	S	Z	N
K	C	A	L	B	A	R	I	K

   red, white, green, yellow, blue, black, orange, brown,
   purple, grey, pink

Pronunciation

6 **b** The <u>ph</u>otogra<u>ph</u>er was on the <u>ph</u>one when the
       <u>f</u>ilm star came through the door, so he missed her.
   c Someone was holding a light but we weren't near
       enou<u>gh</u> to see who it was.
   d They lau<u>gh</u>ed at the sight of the baby ele<u>ph</u>ant
       playing.
   e The sea was very rou<u>gh</u> and we were <u>f</u>rightened.

7 **a** My coat **is** a nice green colour.
   b There was a long queue because it was a
       fashionable restaurant.
   c My brother always wears **shorts** and a T-shirt.
   d I don't wear the same **clothes** every day.
   e My black **trousers are** dirty.
   f She's wearing **a** blue dress.

Unit 15
Grammar

1 **b** mustn't   **c** don't have to   **d** can
   e don't have to   **f** can't   **g** can   **h** must
   i have to   **j** can't

2 **b** don't have to   **c** have to   **d** can't
   e have to   **f** have to   **g** have to   **h** can
   i don't have to   **j** can   **k** can't

3 **c** quietly   **d** correct   **e** nervously   **f** angrily
   g correct   **h** sleepily   **i** miserably   **j** correct
   k happily

Vocabulary

4 **b** get on with   **c** get off   **d** get on
   e get on with

Pronunciation

5 **b** touch   **c** enough   **d** young   **e** dangerous

Exam skills

1 B   2 B

Unit 16
Grammar

1 2 c   3 f   4 a   5 e   6 d

2 **b** join   **c** afraid/sorry   **d** perhaps   **e** come
   f be   **g** What   **h** want   **i** asking   **j** like

3 **b** I'm going to throw away   **c** I'm going to wash
   d I'm going to take   **e** Are you going to paint
   f I'm not going to work   **g** we come
   h I'm going to get   **i** I see
   j Are you going to have
   k I'm not going to decide   **l** we go away

Writing

4 **b** (a) quarter past five *or* five fifteen
   c eight o'clock
   d seventeen minutes past six *or* six seventeen
   e (a) quarter to nine *or* eight forty-five
   f thirteen minutes to seven *or* six forty-seven
   g five to eleven *or* ten fifty-five
   h twenty-five to four *or* three thirty-five

Vocabulary

5

K	N	O	C	K	D	Z	W	E	L	Q	F
T	B	E	W	B	I	A	B	E	P	E	R
C	F	G	J	O	W	L	A	Q	R	J	E
O	L	Q	N	Z	N	P	L	A	E	M	T
R	U	B	B	I	S	H	S	V	L	A	U
G	J	W	C	M	B	O	T	E	A	R	P
A	A	N	F	S	T	B	U	K	X	S	M
N	E	R	S	F	S	Q	U	S	T	H	O
I	D	E	T	N	E	C	S	L	X	A	C
S	M	R	J	E	Y	O	G	E	C	A	B
E	B	R	K	N	R	O	Z	J	I	F	A
D	A	V	V	D	S	L	P	R	I	B	K

knock, relax, computer, organised, rubbish, scented, cool, clubbing, mess

Exam skills

2 far (away) from **3** as/so small as
4 've/have lived **5** are **6** is **7** quickly

Unit 17

Grammar

1 c he will stop **d** Your family will look after
e you come **f** there will not be / won't be
g We will send **h** we receive
i will you arrive **j** will you travel
k Will you need **l** will you stay
m Will you bring **n** you arrive

2 b had her photo taken
c had a garage built
d have their shopping delivered
e will have all my meals cooked
f had our car repaired

3 b anyone **c** someone; anyone **d** Everyone
e no one **f** anyone

Pronunciation

4 b I've been all round the world, but I haven't visited Berlin.
c We can't park here, we'll make a mark on the lawn.
d She's bought an awful card showing a heart and some flowers.
e We aren't poor, because we work hard.

f Would you like half of this burger, or can you eat more?
g He laughed when he saw the bird in the hall.
h They've caught the third burglar.

/ɑ:/ car	/ɔ:/ saw	/ɜ:/ hurt
farm	*Paul*	*return*
can't	all	world
park	lawn	Berlin
mark	bought	work
card	awful	burger
heart	poor	bird
aren't	or	third
hard	more	burglar
half	saw	
laughed	hall	
	caught	

Vocabulary

5

			¹C	O	L	L	E	G	E
²V	A	L	U	E					
		³S	H	A	R	E			
⁴F	L	A	T	M	A	T	E	S	
		⁵B	O	R	R	O	W		
		⁶S	M	A	S	H			
⁷A	C	C	I	D	E	N	T		
		⁸Q	U	A	R	R	E	L	
		⁹F	E	E	S				

Unit 18

Grammar

1 b had changed **c** went **d** had gone
e had read **f** sent **g** phoned **h** had bought

2 b was **c** had never remembered **d** arrived
e had promised **f** opened **g** saw
h had invited **i** had already ordered **j** sang

Vocabulary

3 b reception **c** examination **d** education
e information **f** question **g** direction
h station **i** fiction

Pronunciation

4 aeroplane ✗ answer ✓ appointment ✓
artist ✗ different ✓ doctor ✓ magazine ✗
position ✓ shoulder ✓ story ✓ teacher ✓
tourist ✗ translation ✓ visitor ✓

Exam skills

1 B   2 H   3 D   4 F   5 C

Unit 19

Grammar

1 2 e   3 c   4 g   5 d   6 a   7 f   8 b

2 **b** lets   **c** made   **d** made; didn't let
  e will never let   **f** made; let   **g** let
  h didn't make

Vocabulary

3

			¹U	²N	C	L	E			³H		
⁴C				E				⁵G		⁶M	U	M
O				P				R		S		
U				H				A		B		
⁷S	I	⁸S	T	E	R	-	I	N	-	L	A	W
I		O						D		N		
N		N						F		⁹D	¹⁰A	D
								A			U	
								T			N	
¹¹S	T	E	P	M	O	T	H	E	R		T	
								E				
¹²D	A	U	G	H	T	E	R					

Pronunciation

4 **b** *th* in *thriller* is pronounced /θ/ and *th* in the
  other words is pronounced /ð/
  c *th* in *that* is pronounced /ð/ and *th* in the other
  words is pronounced /θ/
  d *th* in *together* is pronounced /ð/ and *th* in the
  other words is pronounced /θ/

Exam skills

2 A   3 B   4 B   5 A   6 B

Unit 20

Grammar

1 **b** healthily   **c** quickest   **d** slowest
  e better   **f** less quietly

2 **c** The film was so boring (that) I
  switched the TV off.
  d My mum drives so quickly (that) she
  frightens me.
  e She has such long hair (that) it takes hours to
  dry.

f It was so cold (that) I wore two pairs
of socks.
g *Far Planet* is such a good film (that) I want
to see it again.
h The food was so awful (that) I couldn't eat it.
i We have such an old car (that) it often breaks
down.
j This coffee is so strong (that) I can't drink it.

3 **b** or   **c** because   **d** or   **e** but
  f As soon as   **g** so   **h** Although
  i As soon as   **j** so

Pronunciation and spelling

4 **b** there   **c** there   **d** hear   **e** here   **f** hear

Exam skills

2 so tall   3 loudly enough   4 well
5 (the) best/most   6 to come

Unit 21

Grammar

1 **c** Please don't tell   **d** Answer   **e** Don't open
  f Please wave   **g** Please don't phone me

2 **c** to phone the bank
  d Alan not to touch my motorbike
  e Patrick not to go into his office
  f asked Heidi to tidy all the shelves
  g told Alex to give him his jacket

3 Any suitable answers.

4 *Suggested answers*
  b May I speak to Mr Jonas?
  c May I have your name?
  d One moment, please. / Hang on a minute.
  e I'm afraid Mr Jonas isn't available this evening.
  f Can you call back at another time?

5 **a** correct
  b Please call me **on** my mobile.
  c I need a mobile to phone ~~to~~ my parents.
  d correct
  e I rang ~~to~~ the police and told them what
  happened.
  f correct

Vocabulary

6 call back   hang on   hang up   missed call
mobile   ring   switch off   switch on   text
top up

Exam skills

2 D   3 C   4 A   5 B   6 C   7 D
8 A   9 B   10 B

Unit 22

Grammar

1 **c** I don't like
  d I've already spoken
  e I usually keep my phone in my
  f I didn't believe
  g I've seen; I'm

2 **c** he/she'd never heard
  d he'd seen
  e he didn't want
  f she sometimes watched DVDs with her
  g they'd been there; had known about them

Pronunciation

3 **b** ~~science~~ cupboard
  c Although ~~honest~~
  d ~~Who bought~~ Thomas comb
  e brought ~~wrong~~ receipt
  f Where half
  g scissors right ~~wrist~~
  h answered night

Vocabulary

4
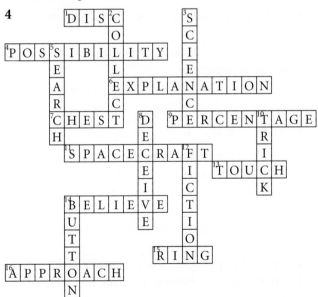

5 **b** prefer   **c** approve   **d** disagree   **e** doubt
  f expect   **g** dislike

Exam skills

Sample answer
Mr Marshall from the garage phoned a few minutes
ago. He said he had received your email but he hadn't
had time to reply because he had been very busy. Can
you phone him please as soon as possible?

Unit 23

Grammar

1 **b** which   **c** where   **d** which   **e** who
  f (which)   **g** (who)   **h** whose
  i where   **j** which

2 **b** who used to live next door
  c (which) we sent to Sarah
  d (which) I enjoyed most
  e who stole my bag
  f (which) I saw yesterday
  g which goes to the airport
  h who gave us directions
  i (which) she's lost
  j which starts at eight

3
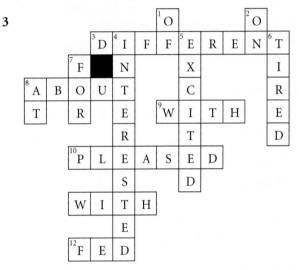

Exam skills

1 A   2 C   3 B

Unit 24

Grammar

1 **b** will be delivered   **c** are cancelled   **d** was paid
  e were woken up   **f** is sent / will be sent
  g will be translated
  h was not / wasn't invited / hadn't been invited
  i is eaten   **j** were offered

2 **b** was asked for my autograph … other fans
  c was interviewed … a newspaper journalist
  d were taken … a famous photographer
  e was driven … my driver
  f was offered champagne … the owner

Vocabulary

3 emergency exit
microwave oven
vacuum cleaner
steam train
shopping trolley
customs officer
electric guitar

4 b thin   c end   d made   e can   f use
 g put   h electric

 It's a toothbrush.

Pronunciation

5 b I bought‿an‿apple pie for my lunch.
 c The museum‿is closed‿on Thursdays.
 d Where‿is your‿other sister today?
 e My name‿is Frank‿and‿I'm‿eighteen
 years‿old.

Exam skills

2 small   3 are   4 will keep   5 of my friends
6 I want

Unit 25

Grammar

1 c Do you want
 d Where did you buy your
 e How much did you pay
 f Will you wear your
 g Can you dance

2 c when he was free
 d whether/if he could speak
 e why he was looking
 f whether/if I had/'d played
 g whether/if she would need

3 b Aphra is sending her father a text.
 c Mahmoud was taking his teacher a letter.
 d Peter will write the manager a letter.
 e Debbie has given Tim the tickets.
 f Joe showed his parents the website.
 g Beth brought her mother a cup of tea.

4 b too many   c enough   d too much
 e too much   f enough   g too many; enough

Vocabulary

5

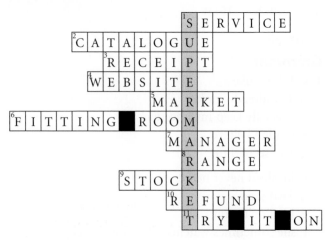

Exam skills

1 B   2 C   3 A   4 C

Unit 26

Grammar

1 b I'll save money on petrol if I buy a smaller car.
 c If you tell anyone my secret, I won't speak to you again.
 d If the teacher cancels the lesson, we'll go to the cinema.
 e We'll leave without them if they don't get here soon.
 f If she moves to that flat, she'll have a long journey to college.
 g I'll help you with your science homework if you teach me Japanese.
 h If he gets the job, he'll earn lots of money.

2 b When   c If   d When   e if
 f When   g if   h if

3 b You won't get a seat at the concert unless you buy a ticket in advance
 c Unless you smile at the customers, you won't get a tip.
 d She'll have to pay a fine unless she takes her library books back today.
 e Unless he apologises, I won't speak to him again.
 f They'll miss the beginning of the film unless they get here soon.

4 1 b   2 a   3 b   4 a

Exam skills
Reading Part 4
1 C 2 B 3 D

Writing Part 1
2 for 3 younger 4 gave 5 big enough
6 go

Unit 27
Grammar
1 b All c Each/Every d all e each
  f each/every g All

2 b enjoyed herself c didn't hurt herself
  d look after themselves e helps herself
  f talks to himself g doesn't he ask himself

Vocabulary
3

A	S	B	C	D	Q	V	E	R	N	L	U	I	O	P
L	U	C	K	I	L	Y	Y	L	L	A	U	T	C	A
S	R	D	F	N	G	I	P	X	A	W	N	E	D	C
K	P	J	H	F	G	F	D	S	A	S	F	P	O	I
C	R	B	N	A	M	I	N	V	F	R	O	T	U	H
F	I	G	H	C	U	K	M	N	B	B	R	D	L	Y
E	S	A	I	T	L	H	J	N	V	U	T	R	S	E
R	I	B	O	X	Y	Y	L	I	K	C	U	L	N	U
U	N	V	G	U	L	S	O	F	I	B	N	O	J	M
S	G	O	F	C	O	U	R	S	E	A	A	D	D	S
A	L	L	I	M	S	A	M	E	N	T	T	C	U	O
W	Y	P	L	L	E	N	Y	R	O	F	E	A	P	M
H	E	L	Y	I	M	U	E	S	K	U	L	T	T	A
U	F	O	R	T	U	N	A	T	E	L	Y	G	Y	N

luckily, actually, surprisingly, in fact, unfortunately,
unluckily, obviously, of course, fortunately

Pronunciation
4 b These are the ch**air**s wh**ere** we were sitting.
  c Th**ere** were t**ear**s in her eyes when she spoke.
  d Our friends are going to sh**are** th**eir** food with us.
  e I don't c**are** if I t**ear** my jeans, th**ey're** very old.
  f W**e're** all feeling ch**eer**ful.
  g I f**ear** th**ere** may be b**ear**s n**ear** h**ere**.

/eə/ fair	/ɪə/ dear
rare	earrings
chairs	tears
where	We're
There	cheerful
share	fear
their	near
care	here
tear	
they're	
there	
bears	

Exam skills
2 A 3 B 4 B 5 A
6 A 7 B 8 B 9 B 10 A

Unit 28
Grammar
1 b If I wasn't/weren't so untidy, I wouldn't lose
    things all the time.
  c I'd/would invite my neighbour to my party if she
    was/were more friendly.
  d If Roseanne found a job, she'd/would have more
    pocket money.
  e If I had a copy of the book you want, I'd/would
    lend it to you.
  f If Amy didn't use a computer, her work would be
    very difficult to read.
  g I'd/would give you all a lift if I owned a bigger car.
  h If I knew the answer, I'd/would tell you.

2 b was/were on Saturday. c cross the border.
  d want to ask any questions. e feels warm.
  f trusted him. g used a diary. h practise hard.

3 b is c would d has e had
  f has g will h has i had j are

Vocabulary
4 b at c by d in e at f at g at
  h on i at j in k by l on m on

5 2 mistake   3 responsible   4 public
   5 qualifications   6 holiday   7 celebrity
   8 nightclub

Exam skills
Sample answer

Dear Sam

It was good to hear from you. I work every Saturday in a supermarket and I earn about £40 a day. I spend it on clothes and going to the cinema with my friends. I think it's important to have a job because you learn about money and you can decide how to spend it. If you get a job, you will have to work very hard in the evenings on your school work. If you don't get a job, you won't be able to do things with your friends at weekends and in the holidays. So I think you should get a job.
I look forward to hearing from you again soon.
Love from …

Unit 29
Grammar
1 b where the beans are?
   c how much steak costs?
   d how I should cook this?
   e if/whether you've got any vegetarian dishes?
   f when strawberries will be available?

2 c Nor do we.   d Nor have I.   e So are we.
   f So will Jane.   g Nor can I.
   h So was the manager.   i Nor has Guy.

Vocabulary
3 2 meal   3 loaf   4 forks   5 salad   6 diet
   7 tomatoes   8 spices   9 sweet   10 tastes
   11 soup   12 picnic

Exam skills
1 H   2 C   3 E   4 B   5 G

Unit 30
Grammar
1 b saw hardly any cars / hardly saw any cars
   c hardly spoke
   d hardly went out
   e learnt hardly anything new / hardly learnt anything (that was) new
   f hardly understood (any of) it / understood hardly any of it

2 b Before leaving home, eat a light meal.
   c Before starting to write, look through the whole paper quickly.
   d Before answering a question, read the text.
   e After completing each part of the exam, check how much time remains.
   f After writing all your answers, read them carefully.
   g After handing in your paper, forget about it and relax!

3 b moved   c lost   d had already started
   e phone   f 've/have owned   g don't hurry

4 a I **do** my homework in my bedroom.
   b I'm living in a hotel **at** the moment.
   c A tourist guide **told** us that the building was very old.
   d We arrived **at** a big lake and had a picnic.
   e She is very **good** at horse-riding.
   f I slept very **badly** in the old bed.
   g I think we will **have** a good time on our holiday.
   h There is a TV so I won't feel **bored** at night.
   i The sun was **shining** in the morning.
   j I **advise** you to choose a big city to visit.
   k I decided to **leave** my friends in the café and go home.
   l He asked me to **go** out with him.
   m I used to **cycle** every day in my country.
   n In winter you can **go** snowboarding or skiing.
   o I hope you ~~to~~ enjoy the party.

Pronunciation
5   *Suggested answers*
   b <u>put</u>   *foot*
   c <u>heard</u>   *bird*
   d <u>down</u>   *round*
   e <u>we're</u>   *near*
   f <u>talk</u>   *hall*
   g <u>key</u>   *be*
   h <u>have</u>   *bag*

Exam skills

Writing Part 1
2 (ever) since   3 which/that   4 like
5 heavy as   6 unless

Writing Part 2

Sample answer

Dear Sara

On Saturday I went to the Bangkok Restaurant with my family. I really enjoyed it because I like Thai food and the waiters were very friendly. Would you like to go there with me next weekend? It's near the station.

Love ...

Acknowledgements

The authors and publishers would like to thank the teachers and students who trialled and commented on the material:

Argentina: Liliana Luna, Claudia Cecilia Muniz, Marite Stringa, Sylvia Trigub; Australia: Jacque Byrne; Brazil: Angela Cristina Antelo Dupont; Cyprus: Peter Lucantoni; France: Virginie Petit, Robert Wright; Italy: James Douglas, Sarah Ellis, Monica Flood; Malta: Matthew Bonnici; Mexico: Jan Isaksen, Universidad Latino-Americano; Spain: Elizabeth Bridges, Samantha Lewis, Nick Shaw; Switzerland: Nancy Hersche, Julia Muller, Jean Rudiger-Harper, Fiona Schmid; United Arab Emirates: Christine Coombe, Philip Lodge, Anne Scullion; UK: Jenny Cooper, Lynda Edwards, Joe Gillespie, Jane Hann, Roger Scott, Tony Triggs; USA: Gregory Manin.

The publishers are grateful to the following for permission to reproduce photographic material:
Alamy for pp 6 /Jim West, 24 /Sally & Richard Greenhill, 26(b) /David White, 38 / Imageshop, 55 /Bubbles Photolibrary, 61(cl) /Picture Partners; Art Directors & TRIP for pp 26(t) /Tibor Bognar, 52 /Spencer Grant; Corbis for p 60 /Tim Pannell; Educationphotos.com for p 32 /John Walmsley; Getty Images for pp 4 /Justin Pumfrey, 14 /Central Press, 15 /Donald Miralle, 18 /David Young-Wolff, 30(*Alma*) /Jon Riley, 30(*Daniela*) /Robert Daly, 34 /Jason Todd, 41 /Dave M. Benett, 42 /Redferns, 48 /Heinz Kluetmeier /Sports Illustrated, 59 /David Barnes, 61(tl) /Tristan Paviot, 61(tr) /Yukmin; Life File Library for p 36 /Jeremy Hoare; Courtesy of NASA for p 46; Photolibrary.com for pp 45 /Andersen Ross, 51 /Wave RF, 61(br), 63 /Goodshoot; Punchstock for pp 22 / Digital vision, 50 /Digital Vision; Reuters for p 25/Jeff Christensen; Rex Features for pp 56 /Rob Cousins/Robert Harding, 61(bl) /OJO Images.

Picture Research by Kevin Brown.

The following photograph was taken on commission:
Trevor Clifford Photography for p 37

We have been unable to trace the copyright holder for the photograph on p 12 and would be grateful for any information to enable us to do so.

Illustrations by Mark Duffin, Nick Duffy, Tony Forbes

The publishers are grateful to Annette Capel and Wendy Sharp for permission to reproduce their original course book concept in *Objective PET* and in all other *Objective* examination course books.